MAINE

FAMILY ADVENTURE GUIDE™

by

ROGER WOODSON

A VOYAGER BOOK

OLD SAYBROOK, CONNECTICUT

Family Adventure Guide is a trademark of The Globe Pequot Press
Cover illustration by Lainé Roundy

Library of Congress Cataloging-in-Publication Data is available.
Woodson, R. Dodge (Roger Dodge), 1955–
Maine : family adventure guide / by Roger Woodson. — 1st ed.
p. cm. — (Family adventure guide series)
"A voyager book."
Includes indexes.
ISBN 0-7627-0039-4
1. Maine—Guidebooks. 2. Family recreation—Maine—Guidebooks.
I. Title. II. Series.
F17.3.W66 1997
917.4104'43—dc21 96-44975
CIP

Manufactured in the United States of America
First Edition/First Printing

DEDICATION

This book is dedicated to Adam, Afton, and Kimberley, the people who make fun family travel possible for me.

ACKNOWLEDGMENTS

I'd like to acknowledge my parents, Maralou and Woody, for taking me on trips when I was young. They got me started early and I haven't stopped yet.

MAINE

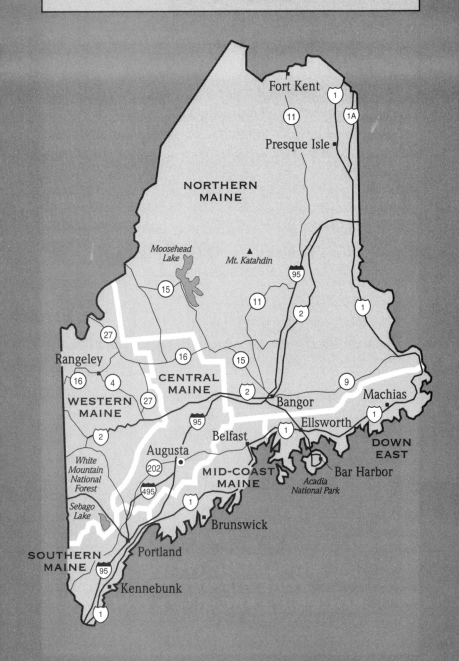

Fort Kent
1
11
1A
Presque Isle

NORTHERN
MAINE

Moosehead
Lake
Mt. Katahdin
95

15
11
2
1

27
15
Rangeley
16
CENTRAL
MAINE
2
9
Machias
16
4
27
2
Bangor
1
WESTERN
MAINE
95
1
Ellsworth
DOWN
EAST
2
Belfast
1
Augusta
202
MID-COAST
MAINE
Bar Harbor
White
Mountain
National
Forest
495
Acadia
National Park
1
Sebago
Lake
1
Brunswick
Portland
SOUTHERN
MAINE
95
1
Kennebunk

CONTENTS

INTRODUCTION

A visit to Maine is something you and your children are not likely to ever forget. Ocean waves break on white beaches along the coast, majestic mountains rise toward the heavens in Jackman, and the people who live and work in Maine are warm and friendly. I moved to Maine, from Virginia, many years ago and have lived here ever since. My children, Afton and Adam, were born in Maine, and they love the state. There is so much to do, and there's something for everyone in every season.

Why should you vacation in Maine? Well, you might decide to spend time in the North Woods, where moose outnumber year-round residents or antiques shops and cozy harbor towns might be what pull you to Vacationland. Of course, you can't forget the beaches and the lobsters that are famous when it comes to Maine. Lakes are plentiful in the area, and you've got your choice of lodging, from luxurious accommodations to rustic cabins. If you want fun, variety, and plenty to do, Maine's the place to do it.

When you are planning a vacation, Maine has more to offer than you will have time to experience. You can shop till you drop at outlet stores in Kittery and Freeport, take a whitewater rafting ride out of The Forks, or just relax on a quiet lake where the only sound you hear is the call of a loon.

Maine is a state that is geared towards tourists. Without tourist traffic, the economy in Maine would be devastated. This means that people are going to cater to your needs and desires with every interest in pleasing you. I can't think of a better place to spend a few weeks away from work. My vacations to Maine turned into an obsession to move to the state, and ultimately, I made the move. After more than a decade of living and working in Maine, I have no regrets and plenty of good memories. Come on, come to Maine and make your own memories.

Now that you've decided that Maine is the place of your dreams, use this book as your hometown guide. Having two children and living in Maine has prompted me to explore the many wonderful opportunities that are available, and I'm going to share them with you and your family. From the moment you cross the bridge into the state of Maine to the time you reach your final destination, this book will give you all the help you need in planning your route, your agenda, and in many cases, your budget. It's hard to imagine a place better suited for fun and relaxation than Maine.

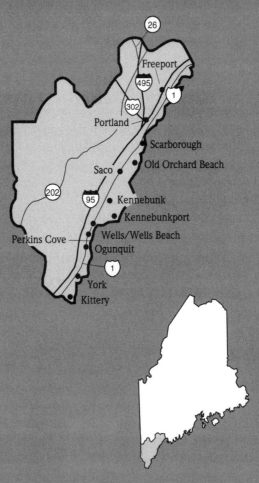

Southern Maine

Southern Maine

outhern Maine has much to offer travelers. You can swim at one of the numerous beaches, shop in outlet stores, stroll through picturesque harbor towns, enjoy amusement parks, and much, much more. Maine deserves its nickname of Vacationland, and southern Maine is only the beginning of a diverse and delightful adventure when you choose to explore the Pine Tree State.

KITTERY

Kittery is the gateway to Maine. When you drive across the bridge that spans the Piscataqua River, you will leave New Hampshire and be welcomed to Maine. Once in the state, you will have immediate access to **outlet stores** for Maine-made and famous-brand goods. You can count on seeing nearly 100 outlet stores that sell everything from shoes to skis.

If you've had enough of outlet goods, a must-see attraction is the **Kittery Trading Post** (207–439–2700). Your children will marvel at the larger-than-life chain-saw carvings of pioneers. Racks of clothes, canoes, unbelievable amounts of sporting goods, and much more are all at this one store. You can buy fishing gear, picnic items, or souvenirs. Kids love to play in the tents that are set up in the camping area, and there are many natural history exhibits for your children to enjoy. Open Monday through Saturday from 9:00 A.M. to 9:00 P.M. and Sunday from 10:00 A.M. to 6:00 P.M., the

Kittery Trading Post offers three floors of outdoor recreational equipment, clothing, and footwear. (Courtesy Kittery Trading Post)

Trading Post maintains a prominent position on U.S. Route 1 in Kittery.

Right across the street from the trading post is a favorite restaurant of tourists and locals alike. It's the **Weathervane** (207–439–0330). People who enjoy seafood love the Weathervane. Special deals are on the menu for children, and the food is fantastic. While seafood is the specialty here, burgers and fries and other entrees are offered for people who like their food to come from dry land. If you want down-home cooking in the Maine tradition, you have to eat at the Weathervane. Prices are moderate.

You could bypass most of Kittery by staying on I–95, but you should-n't. Stick to U.S. Route 1 for a more enjoyable and much more scenic trip. Seeing lobster traps, buoys, and other colorful Maine icons is an important part of your family adventure. The shops, stores, and people of Kittery are well worth the time you spend exploring them. After all, Kittery is Maine's oldest town.

Kittery is steeped in tradition as the state's early center of shipbuilding. The **Kittery Historical and Naval Museum** on U.S. Route 1 near its intersection with Route 236; 207–439–3080) traces this region's maritime history. This museum is open Monday through Friday from 10:00 A.M. to 4:00 P.M. from June 1 through October 31. Paul Jones' ship, the *Ranger,* which was launched in the Piscataqua River in 1777, is on display here.

Kittery Point, which is southeastward of Kittery on Route 103, offers winding roads, ocean vistas, and austere eighteenth-century houses for your viewing pleasure. Your children might get a kick out of seeing the forts here. **Fort McClary**, known earlier as Fort Williams, can be explored. Built in 1715, this fort has proved crucial to the area's defense. Expanded during the American Revolution, the War of 1812, and the Civil War, the fort also underwent further changes during the 1898 Spanish-American War. The most memorable aspect of this landmark is the hexagonal wooden blockhouse built in 1844 and reputed to be the last blockhouse built in Maine. Hours of operation are 10:00 A.M. to 5:00 P.M. daily, except for Wednesdays. Picnic tables are available here if you and your family want to bring a lunch and eat outdoors to enjoy the beautiful views.

Fort Foster, also in the area of Fort McClary, is now a municipal park on Gerrish Island, which is accessible by bridge, just off Route 103, north of Kittery Point Village. The park offers swimming from pebble beaches, fishing, a ball field, picnic spots, and nature trails. During its active use as a military defense post, Fort Foster anchored one end of a submerged net that was intended to keep prowling German submarines from spying on the Portsmouth Naval Yard. A fee of $2.00 per vehicle plus $1.00 per adult and $.50 per child is charged for admission to the park. Hours of operation are 10:00 A.M. to 8:00 P.M.

Restaurants and lodging are plentiful in the Kittery area. **Bob's Clam Hut** on Route 1 in Kittery (207–439–4233) is a favorite spot of locals who enjoy outstanding fried clams. You too can stop by here at any time of the year. If you're after something a bit fancier, try **Cap'n Simeon's Galley** (207–439–3655) on Route 103 in Pepperel Cove. It offers views that are sure to make leaving difficult. Part of this restaurant was built in 1680 as the original Frisbee Store. Most visitors opt for seafood, the specialty of the house, but you can also get sandwiches, burgers, quiche, salads, steak, and other fare. Prices are reasonable and fit for a large family.

Breakfast couldn't be better than what you will enjoy at **The Line House** (207–439–3401) on Route 1 at the Kittery-York town line. This restaurant is open all year and serves eggs in more ways that you can imagine. Lunch and dinner are also available, with meals ranging from seafood platters to liver and onions. Children are welcome and can enjoy their own portions and specials.

As you drive north from Kittery on Route 1, a multitude of lodging is available on each side of the road. Bed and breakfasts in the area often restrict the age of children that may stay in the facilities. Some don't allow children at all. **Enchanted Nights Bed and Breakfast** (207–439–1489) is rare in that it allows both children and pets. Located at 29 Wentworth Street in Kittery, this is one of the best bed and breakfasts available to families. The **Blue Roof Motel** (207–439–9324) on Route 1 Bypass also caters to children and pets. **Super 8 Motel** (207–439–2000; 85 Route 1 Bypass) is also happy to have your family and pets. Other facilities in the area that allow children include the **Coachman Motor Inn** (380 Route 1; 800–824–6183), **Northeaster Motel** (79 Old Post Road; 207–439–0116), and the **Rex Motel** (90 Route 1 Bypass; 207–439–9002).

YORK

Just up the road from Kittery you'll find York, which is made up of four communities: York Village, York Harbor, York Beach, and Cape Neddick. From Memorial Day to Labor Day, the four communities are linked even more closely through a trolleybus service to all the villages. It operates daily from 10:00 A.M. to 5:00 P.M.

Founded in the 1600s, York offers visitors a taste of yesteryear. Many of the old homes and buildings are open for public inspection. Take a spin down Lindsay Road, which runs between York Street and the York River, to get a glimpse of the York Historic District.

Among the buildings in this district is **Jefferds Tavern,** a watering hole for travelers as far back as 1759, when it was built in the town of Wells. The tavern was moved to York in 1942. You can buy tickets that allow you to explore the tavern as well as six other buildings that make up the Old York Historical Society. History comes to life as you

ROGER'S FAVORITE FAMILY ADVENTURES IN SOUTHERN MAINE

York Wild Kingdom Zoo and Amusement Park, York;
   207–363–4911
Wells Recreation Area, Wells; 207–646–2939
Rachel Carson National Wildlife Refuge, Wells; 207–646–9226
Aquaboggan, Saco; 207–282–3112
Cascade Water and Amusement Park, Saco; 207–284–6231
Funtown U.S.A., Saco; 207–284–5139
Maine Aquarium, Saco; 207–284–4512
Palace Playland, Old Orchard Beach; 207–934–2001
Scarborough Marsh, Scarborough; 207–883–5100
The Village Park Family Entertainment Center,
   Old Orchard Beach; 207–934–7666
Desert of Maine, Freeport; 207–865–6962

tour the tavern, the **Emerson-Wilcox house, the Elizabeth Perkins House, the Old Schoolhouse, the Old Gaol, the George A. Marshall Stone Building,** and the **John Hancock Warehouse.** Exhibits created by the historical society bring to life the living conditions of early York residents.

Your children may also enjoy making rubbings of early tombstones at the **Old Burying Ground** in the same district. The Old Gaol was built in 1719 and used until 1860 as a jail for debtors and criminals. Fieldstone walls surrounding this building are 2 feet thick. In 1900 the jail was converted to a museum, and the cells, dungeon, and gaoler's quarters are furnished as they might have been around 1790.

Tickets can be purchased at Jefferds Tavern at a cost of $6.00 for adults and $2.50 for children. The buildings open to the public around mid-June and remain active through September. Hours of operation are 10:00 A.M. to 5:00 P.M. Tuesday through Saturday and 1:00 to 5:00 P.M. on Sunday. Call (207) 363–4974 for information. If old buildings don't suit your fancy, consider trying the beaches that are just up the road.

Long Sands Beach stretches from York Harbor to Cape Neddick and is accessible from Route 1A. The beach stretches 2 miles and houses Cape Neddick Light. Locals know this lighthouse best as Nubble Light. Artists and photographers are drawn to Nubble Light in much the same way a moth is pulled toward a light bulb. The beach is a wonderful diversion for kids who are tired of riding in the family car. Your children can explore the coarse, grey sand and the nooks and crannies of this shore while enjoying the playful action of soaring gulls.

The gulls are native to Maine, but you might want to investigate some more exotic birds and animals at the **York Wild Kingdom Zoo and Amusement Park** (207–363–4911), a big hit with kids and adults. To get to the zoo take exit 2 off I–95, turn right on Route 9 to Route 1 north. You'll see the zoo on the right with a large sign. Professional photographers come to the zoo to capture exotic animals on film in natural settings. This facility houses Maine's only white tiger. Children enjoy petting deer and handling friendly snakes. They can also feed and pet goats, marvel at prairie dogs, be mesmerized by monkeys, and laugh at lions. If you and the kids are lucky, a camel will spit on you. It's said to bring good luck. Elephant rides are big business here, as are the pony rides.

In addition to the animals, the Wild Kingdom Zoo facility also has paddleboats, a gift shop, shows and demonstrations, and a small playground. A centrally located snack bar can help you put hunger behind you, and the well-kept grounds provide places to rest and relax.

If animals don't quite meet your energy or interest levels, you can spend most of your time in the complex's amusement park. Rides, games, and other entertainments typical of carnivals are here.

An excellent place for the whole family, the entire complex opens in May and closes in September. Hours vary with the passage of the seasons, but opening time is usually 10:00 A.M. and closing is between 5:00 and 6:00 P.M. Fees for the zoo only are $9.95 for adults and children aged eleven and up; $7.75 for children aged two to ten; and free for kids under the age of two. Combo tickets for the zoo and amusement park cost $12.75 for adults and children over ten, kids between the ages of four and ten pay $9.50, and $3.50 for children three and under. Parking is plentiful and free.

A landmark in York Beach is **The Goldenrod** restaurant (207–363–2621). Located in the heart of York Beach, The Goldenrod has been around for 100 years. You can watch saltwater taffy kisses being made, have lunch in their dining room, and splurge on homemade ice cream, and then explore their gift shop. Open from Memorial Day to Labor Day, The Goldenrod is within walking distance from the beach.

Another must see in York Beach is the **Surfside Fun-o-rama**, an old arcade located right across from the beach. The games inside range from the computer enhanced to the prehistoric and the building, with its high ceilings and creaky wood floors, is reminiscent of bygone days. Save up your quarters for this great rainy day stop. Open from Memorial Day to Labor Day.

OGUNQUIT AND PERKINS COVE

If you are traveling north on U.S. Route 1, plan to spend some time in the **Ogunquit** area. Consider driving up the Shore Road (off Route 1 in Ogunquit). It provides scenery that has to be seen to be believed. The village of **Perkins Cove** will be encountered as you pass through Ogunquit's southern end. This picturesque spot was once home to fishermen and artists. Restaurants, shops, cafes, galleries, and similar attractions now consume most of the real estate, and parking can be a problem. But, it's hard to imagine a spot that feels more like Maine than Perkins Cove. Artists still perch upon the water-worn rocks and bring their canvas alive with images of a salty seaport.

As you walk the streets of this tourist town, you will be surrounded by dozens of shops offering everything from jewelry to crafts. Our family's favorites are **Golden Sails, Cove's End, The Country Shop,** and the **Strawberry Bazaar.** If you or your kids have a sweet tooth, visit **Ayla's Sweet Shop. The Artist's Gallery** and **Ocean Winds Art Gallery** are good places to look for something to take home with you.

An institution of Perkins Cove is **Barnacle Billy's** (207–646–5575) restaurant, sitting on a rocky point of land at the water's edge. Other family-friendly restaurants include **The Lobster Shack** (207–646–2941), the **Oar Weed Cove** (207–646–4022), **Jackie Too** (207–646–4444), and **Hurricane** (207–646–6348). If you're looking for something light and fast, try the **Riverbank Cafe** or the **Blue Willow**. All of these are located along the main route in Perkins Cove.

You and your children can venture out on the pedestrian drawbridge that spans the harbor entrance. If you're lucky, a large sailboat will blow its horn to request the raising of the bridge when you are nearby. This is done with a series of buttons, and it's common for the nearest person to the drawbridge keeper to become honorary operator of the bridge. Kids get a real kick out of this.

Water-related activities are abundant in Perkins Cove. For sightseeing trips or fishing trips, bring your deck shoes and hop a boat to take in all the salty air you can stand. Try **Finestkind Scenic Cruises** at (207) 646–5227 if you would like to go out on a lobster fishing excursion or take a cruise by Nubble Light for some breathtaking photo opportunities. Cruises run from mid-May to mid-October and prices range from $8.00 to $13.00 for adults and $6.00 to $9.00 for children. Some cruises may be more. If deep-sea fishing is more your style, the ***Bunny Clark*** at (207) 626–2214 or the ***Ugly Anne*** at (207) 646–7202 can fix you right up. Be prepared to see whales and seals as you drift over the wild Atlantic. From the end of April to Labor Day half-day cruises are $30 per person. From Labor Day to Columbus day you can take a full-day cruise for $45 per person.

When you are moving about on dry land, your feet are your best friend. Traffic and parking can be a serious problem in this popular tourist town. If you don't feel like walking, you can take advantage of the local trolley. Each time you board, it costs $.50 per person. The service runs from late May through Columbus Day from 8:00 A.M. to 9:00 P.M. in the fringe season and 8:00 A.M. to 11:00 P.M. between July 1 and Labor Day. You can call the Ogunquit Chamber of Commerce at (207) 646–2939 for more information.

When you leave Perkins Cove on the Shore Road and continue northward toward Ogunquit, stop at the **Marginal Way.** This favorite footpath stretches for a mile along the shore between the two villages. Artists of all

Ogunquit Beach is definitely a "beautiful place by the sea." (Courtesy Maine Office of Tourism)

types flock here for inspiration. The walk is beautiful as you weave your way along granite cliffs and look down on crashing surf. The trail begins next to the Sparhawk Resort on Shore Road in downtown Ogunquit.

Children enjoy the tidal pools that can be explored as you walk this path that once served as a cattle highway. A farmer, Josiah Chase, gave the Marginal Way to the town of Ogunquit in 1923. In doing this, he preserved a right of way to drive cattle down the path and around rocky Israel's Head each summer to graze on the marsh grass in Wells. Parking for this path is difficult to find, but check around the mini-lighthouse on Israel's Head and at the town police station on Cottage Street.

Ogunquit Beach is another wonderful destination. It sprawls out over 3 miles of sand and surf. As you see the dunes, you might think that the weaving sea grass is beckoning you to visit. Abenaki Indians named this region appropriately: The translation of Ogunquit is "beautiful place by the sea." The most popular access to this beach is from the foot of Beach Street. Your kids can get a snack along the boardwalk, change into swimming gear, or use the restrooms along the way. A parking lot is available with rates of $2.00 per hour per vehicle.

Another means of reaching Ogunquit Beach is the **Footbridge Beach** access. You arrive here by taking Ocean Street off Route 1, about 1 mile north of the center of Ogunquit. This access is less crowded and offers restrooms for visitors. Parking is available at a rate of $6.00 per vehicle per day. **Moody Beach** also offers an entrance to Ogunquit Beach, Eldridge Street off Route 1 in Wells is the road to take for this access. Parking is $6.00 a day per vehicle. Moody Beach is private property above the high-water mark, so don't stray onto sections where you may get into trouble with landowners and police.

If you have a taste for the dramatic arts, you might consider taking the family to **Ogunquit Playhouse** (207–646–5511) on Route 1 in Ogunquit. For more than six decades, dramas, comedies, and musicals have all been staged here. Broadway talent makes the Ogunquit Playhouse one of the most popular theaters in the state. June 26 is the usual opening night of this summer theater. Evening shows run Monday through Saturday; curtain is at 8:30 P.M. Afternoon matinees are scheduled on Wednesdays and Thursdays at 2:30 P.M.

WELLS

Wells, Maine, was settled in 1640. Sixty-two square miles of land provide space for its 9,000 year-round residents, who live in named sections that combine to form the town. Moody Beach accounts for the southern coastal area, Wells Beach is part of the make-up, and Drakes Island is the most northerly beach. The western end is flanked by sections called High Pine, Wells Branch, and Merriland Ridge.

Great family fun in Wells can begin in the **Wells Recreation Area** situated along Route 9A. This seventy-acre playground for young and old alike includes four asphalt tennis courts, two basketball courts, and a baseball diamond among other attractions. Picnic tables welcome visitors, while those interested in staying fit can work out along a 2-mile fitness course. The sound of horseshoes clanking together can be heard as good sports try to ring the peg. A dirt track surrounding the perimeter of an all-purpose sports field provides a place for walking and running.

Visitors here can also enjoy **Hobb's Pond,** adjacent to the recreation area. A dock is provided for visitors to use in launching their own canoes and kayaks. Children will want to spend hours on the massive playground, and adults will welcome the fresh Maine air as they take a breather during their busy vacations. Call the Wells Recreation Department Office at (207) 646–5826 for more information.

For more outdoor fun, Wells has three miniature golf courses, all on Route 1. **Wells Beach Mini-Golf** is right next to **Big Daddy's Ice Cream,** making a handy combination for families. **Wonder Mountain** is a mini-golf course complete with waterfalls. **Sea-Vu Mini Golf** is another place to tee up a ball.

When putting around isn't appealing, you can turn your attention to fishing. **Wells Harbor** is an ideal place to rent some fishing tackle and bait. You and your kids can fish from a municipal dock or from harbor jetties. Surf casting is available near the mouth of the Mousam River. A variety of fish inhabit these waters, so every tug on the line can bring in a surprise.

If rain forces you inside, consider some of the local museums; the following ones are great for families.

The Museum at Historic First Meeting House on Route 1 is open daily from June to October. Winter hours are offered on Thursdays only. Hours vary with different days of the week, but, no matter when you visit, the museum's artifacts, memorabilia, and genealogies of early Wells residents shed light on this historic seacoast town. The Wells Chamber of Commerce can provide more information on this (and other attractions in Wells). Call the chamber at (207) 646–2451.

The **Wells Auto Museum** (1181 Post Road [which is Route 1]; 207–646–9064), holds more than seventy antique automobiles. Among them you can see a 1955 Chrysler 300A, a 1918 Stutz Berarcat, and a 1941 Packard Convertible. Antique car rides are part of the fun here, and most children enjoy the sensation of a jaunt in a Model-T Ford. If your kids don't like cars, the chances are good that they will stay entertained with the museum's arcade games and nickelodeons while the adults enjoy the exhibits. A gift shop holds treasures for souvenir collectors.

The price of admission is $3.50 for adults and $2.00 for kids six through twelve. The Wells Auto Museum is open on weekends only in May and October from 10:00 A.M. to 5:00 P.M., and at the same hours daily from mid-June to mid-September.

When the skies clear, you can take a quick historical tour of the monuments that stand in memory of Wells' past. Visit the Meetinghouse Museum (207–646–4775) on Route 1 to learn details. A trip to Storer Park on Route 1 will turn up a monument depicting a battle between the French and Indians and the early Wells residents. Wells' twenty-four valiant settlers were vastly outnumbered during this battle, but they managed to resist 400 of their enemy. Other markers can be found within the town. A complete list can be obtained by contacting the town hall at (207) 646–5113, or the Wells Historical Society at (207) 646–4775. This is a good opportunity to give your kids a chance to explore history and mystery as you take a walking or driving tour.

Also perfect for a day outdoors is the **Rachel Carson National Wildlife Refuge** at 321 Post Road, Route 9. When completely open, it will contain 7,435 acres of salt marsh and upland habitat. Early settlers relied on this marshland for harvesting salt-marsh hay, and the dikes constructed by these old-timers can still be seen. Today the refuge provides a home to more than 250 species of birds—a bird's and a bird-watcher's paradise. A 1-mile nature trail has been made for people limited to wheelchair travel. The trail is accessible from Route 9, just off Route 1. To obtain further information, call (207) 646–9226.

One place you can't pass up if you and your children have any interest in nature and the environment is the **Wells National Estuarine Research Preserve** at Laudholm Farm (342 Laudholm Farm Road; 207–646–1555). Dedicated to preservation and research, its 1,600 acres encompass fields, forest, wetlands, and beach area. Three rivers—the Merriland, Webhannet, and Little—meet the ocean on this property, creating a rich estuarine habitat for wildlife. Many endangered species call this reserve home. Black ducks, least terns, peregrine falcons, and piping plovers are the most noted residents. Native wildflowers like arethus and slender blue flag can be seen on the premises.

The heart of this reserve is Laudholm Farm, a historic saltwater farm that allows visitors to view nature at its best. Whether your interest is cultural history, natural history, or just a day of fun, this is one place you must visit. Many exhibits, programs, and trail sessions are open to the public, and children thrill at exploring the reserve with Annie Otter, Mitchell Mummichog, and other special family tour guides. One section of the reserve includes five trails used in the children's Discovery Program. Junior researchers (kids between the ages of nine and eleven) can attend day camps that last a full four days. Older children (between eleven and thirteen) can participate in their own special research program.

Family tours give children a chance to exercise their senses of sight and smell along the trails laced throughout this reserve. Guides and instructors instigate hands-on learning. When the tides are agreeable, your children can explore the intertidal rock pools on Laudholm Beach. Scud, crabs, and snails are common finds in these tidal-pool explorations.

If you're up for an easy walk along a 7-mile trail, you can take an hour-and-a-half guided tour to see the watersheds of the Little River and the Webhannet estuaries. Birds, flowers, and butterflies command a great deal of attention on this walk. Orchids are the star players of the wildflowers. Butterflies hover over milkweed, and bees visit snapdragons. Ferns are abundant. Any trip into the flowering section of the reserve is sure to evoke long-lasting memories.

A special program called Skywatch offers night visitors a chance to use telescopes in their hunt for meteor showers and lunar eclipses. The Full-Moon Walk puts you in touch with wildlife that is seldom seen. Deer may be caught grazing in the glow of a full moon, or you might see and hear the nearly silent swoop of an owl.

History buffs will be interested to learn how this Native American encampment area came to be a wildlife reserve. Colonial highways, Indian shutters, antique weathervanes, and turn-of-the-century buildings are only part of what you will discover here about this slice of American history.

Arriving at the Wells Reserve is easy. Take the Maine Turnpike north to Exit 2. Turn left onto Route 9 and continue until you reach traffic lights at U.S. Route 1. Turn left and continue again for 1.5 miles. Turn right at the second blinking light onto Laudholm Farm Road. Then, turn left at the fork and right into the reserve. There is no admission fee, but a guided tour can be taken for $2.50 a person. A $5.00 fee is charged for parking in July and August. Call for complete details, but don't pass up this exciting opportunity.

After a full day of exploring, you may feel the need for a place to bed down for the night. You'll be able to rest easy: Lodging in the Wells area is plentiful and diverse. The Wells Chamber of Commerce can supply a full listing of all such options; call them at (207) 646–2451, or consider some of the following suggestions.

If you favor your own cottage, contact **Water Crest Cottages and Motel** at (800) 847–4693. You can rent a one- or two-bedroom cottage, complete with a modern kitchen, screened porch, and air conditioning. A heated pool and spa are added incentives for staying here.

Campers can contact **Stadig Campground** at (207) 646–2298. The facility is just 2 miles north of Wells on the Route 1 Bypass. This campground opens on Memorial Day and closes on October 1. Another camping option is **Beach Acres** (563 Eldredge Road, off Route 1; 207–646–5612). This facility offers seasonal camping between Memorial Day and early October, with regular camping kicking in from Memorial Day to Labor Day. Beach Acres is situated less than a mile from a beach. You can swim, enjoy the on-site playground, play shuffleboard, or picnic. A twenty-four-hour security guard is on duty, and fireplaces and a laundromat are available. Pets are not allowed.

You can rough it in comfort at **East Winds Vacation Resort** (371 Mile Road, Wells Beach; 800–638–3366). Located within easy walking distance of a beach, this facility offers furnished rooms, fully functional kitchens (including dishwashers, garbage disposals, and microwaves), heat, air conditioning, cable television, phones, and carport parking. Each room accommodates four adults. Rates run about $100 per room. Other affordable family lodging in the area can be found at **Seagull Motor Inn** (Route 1; 207–646–5164 or 800–573–2485) and **Wonderview Motor Village** (Route 1; 207–646–2304). Prices begin at $69 per room.

So many fine food establishments are in the Wells area that you owe it to yourself to contact the Wells Chamber of Commerce (at the same telephone number above) for a full listing. You can also venture to some of the places mentioned in the next paragraphs.

Meals at **Billy's Chowder House** (207–646–7558) at 216 Mile Road in Wells are made with fresh seafood, including lobster. Steak and cocktails are also available. Opening annually in mid-January, Billy's doesn't close down until mid-December. The **Bull and Claw** restaurant on

U.S. Route 1 boasts of their fun family dining and their pledge to serve so much to so many for so little. Their breakfast and brunch buffet is not to be missed. Major credit cards are welcome. You can make plans for a meal at the Bull and Claw by calling (207) 646–8467.

The **Grey Gull Inn** (475 Webhannet Drive; 207–646–7501) at Moody Point in Wells puts on a fancy feed, but the prices tend to be a little high for large families. Prime rib, broiled haddock, pasta, and other entrees fill the menu here. **Litchfield's** (207–646–5711) on Route 1 in Wells is a favorite dining spot for natives. House specialties include Aztec chicken and prime rib. Seafood is also readily available at affordable prices. Many locals rave about the lunch sandwiches served here.

If you got up early and feel in the mood for a breakfast muffin, pastries, or doughnuts, give **Congdon's Donuts Family Restaurant** a try. Located on Route 1 in Wells, Condon's is open at 6:30 A.M. and continues to serve until 2:00 P.M. In addition to scrumptious muffins, breads, and pastries, you can get ice cream made right on the premises.

The Hayloft (207–646–4400), located on Route 1 (at Bourne Rd.) in Moody, is open all year-round and is a great family stop. Their specialty is delicious "broasted" chicken and homemade deserts. Open 11:00 A.M. to 9:00 P.M.

KENNEBUNK

You can arrive at **Kennebunk** by driving north from Wells on Route 1 or Interstate 95. If you're on the interstate highway, take Exit 3. Home now to some 8,000 residents, this town was originally founded at Cape Porpoise. In past centuries the area supported a thriving fishing and shipbuilding industry.

Today, **Summer Street** is often walked by visitors interested in seeing the homes of past sea captains. **The Brick Store Museum** at 117 Main Street (207–985–4802) is a favorite stopping point for those who wish to look back in time. The museum exhibits will take you and your children to the Revolutionary War era. Hours are Tuesday through Friday, 10:00 A.M. to 4:30 P.M., year-round. From April 15 to December 15, it's open Saturday, 10:00 A.M. to 4:30 P.M. Admission for adults is $3.00; children pay $2.00.

Recreation in the area includes **Gooch's Beach** and **Kennebunk**

Beach. Both beaches are reached from Beach Avenue. Tidal pools are a favorite attraction on these beaches, but picnicking is prohibited. Parking is limited, and permits are required. Permits can be obtained from the town hall on weekdays or from local lodging facilities. Kennebunk Beach has a reputation as a family beach.

The Nature Conservancy property (14 Main Street; 207–729–5181) offers 1,500 acres of blueberry fields and nature trails.

If you want to stroll through stores, spend some time at **Lafayette Center** at Storer and Maine Streets. This converted shoe factory houses a host of upscale shops. The **Brick Store Exchange** at 4 Dane Street showcases locally crafted items. In addition, you can discover antiques shops and art galleries are abundant in the Kennebunk region. For more information, call the chamber of commerce at (207) 967–0857.

Special treats in Kennebunk include souvenir shops, 211 adorable inns along the beach area, and gourmet-class restaurants. **The Sundial Inn** (48 Beach Avenue; 207–967–3850), for example, is placed at the ocean's edge. This turn-of-the-century inn provides fabulous rooms furnished with country Victorian antiques. Open all year, the Sundial Inn is representative of the quality accommodations and service you will enjoy in the Kennebunk region. Prices range from $80 in the off season to $150 in season. There is a three-night minimum stay mid-summer.

Lake Brook B&B Guest House (207–967–4069; 57 Western Avenue, Lower Village) in Kennebunk is a fine place for families to stay. This turn-of-the-century farmhouse is completed by a large, wraparound porch with a view of the salt marsh and tidal brook. Suites are available in July and August. If you want to be on the water, check out **The Ocean View** (72 Beach Avenue; 207–967–2750). This facility offers breakfast in bed to guests occupying suites. The rates are a little steep ($130 to $170), but you should treat yourself to a few luxuries during your trip.

If you and your gang are feeling hungry, try **The Impastable Dream** (17 Maine Street; 207–985–4290) in Kennebunk. Open daily, except Sunday, from 11:00 A.M. to 8:00 P.M., it has an Italian menu. You will be awed by the pine floors and stenciling while you wait for a meal that will leave you with no room for dessert.

KENNEBUNKPORT

Kennebunkport doesn't boast a large population—only about 3,300 residents live here year-round—but it is a summer retreat home to former president George Bush. Built in 1903, the Bush home is at **Walker's Point** on Ocean Avenue. **Dock Square** is the hot spot of Kennebunkport. Books have been written about this lively slice of Maine, and to this day, people come from all around to celebrate summer at Dock Square.

For adventure out of the center of town, head to the beaches. **Goose Rocks Beach** on Route 9 just north of Kennebunkport is a quiet, out-of-the-way beach that attracts windsurfers, but parking is limited. **Parson's Beach** and **Crescent Surf Beach,** both on Parson's Beach Road, are popular with bird-watchers. A white, sandy beach and salt marshes make these nice settings for family fun, but no facilities and limited parking keep crowds at a minimum. All of the beaches in this area are suitable for swimming, but the water is cold until well into the summer season. If the weather, and the water temperature conspire to shorten your visit to the beaches, plenty of other activities await you in the Kennebunkport area.

For instance, the **Seashore Trolley Museum** (207–967–2712) contains more than 200 transit vehicles waiting for your inspection. Located on Log Cabin Road, the museum is open from May to October; the hours vary, so it's best to call ahead. You and your family can ride on a restored electric trolley that takes you for a 4-mile run through woods and fields. Admission is $6.00 per person. People who prefer to spend their time on the water will appreciate the *Elizabeth 2* (207–967–5595). From May through October, you and your family can take a 1 1/2-hour cruise on the *Elizabeth 2* to gain a great deal of insight on the cultural and natural history of the area, not to mention some great views. The trip begins at the dock behind the Mobil gas station that is next to the bridge on Route 9.

Some serious golf can be played in Kennebunkport. **The Cape Arundel Golf Club** (207–967–3494) often accommodates the golfing requirements of former president George Bush. This eighteen-hole course is open to the public except from 11:00 A.M. to 2:30 P.M. from mid-June to mid-September. **Webhannet Golf Club** (207–967–2061) provides eighteen holes of challenging golf. Public golfers are welcome except from 11:30 A.M. to 1:00 P.M. Another course that is worth a look is the **Dutch Elm**

Golf Course (207–282–9850) in the town of **Arundel.**

If your kids are too young for golf or not into the game, go out to watch some whales. Kennebunkport is the perfect jumping-off spot for **whale watching.** Whales are frequent visitors to the feeding grounds at **Jeffrey's Ledge,** about 20 miles offshore. Species seen include finbacks, minkes, rights, and humpbacks. The seas can be rough, so take precautions for anyone who is prone to seasickness. Two boats specialize in getting people to the whales; they are the ***Nautilus*** (207–967–0707) and the ***Indian Whale Watch*** (207–967–5912).

Food is never far away when you are in Kennebunkport. Many restaurants cater to adults with healthy budgets, but you can find plenty of places to eat less expensively with the kids. **Windows on the Water** (207–967–3313) at Chase Hill can feed you for less than $10 a plate. Reservations are required for dinner but not for lunch. **Breakwater Restaurant and Inn** (207–967–3118) has some afford-able fare. It is located at Ocean Avenue. **Seascapes** (77 Pier Road, Cape Porpoise; 207–967–8500) is a favorite place to eat because of its location. You and your family will dine on a working fishing pier while enjoying seafood at prices that will not require a second mortgage on your home.

Bartley's Dockside (207–967–5050) offers candlelight dining by the fire with a water view. This establishment is famous for its chowder, and the prices are reasonable. **Mabel's Lobster Claw** (207–967–2562) is one of George Bush's hangouts. Lobster is the food of choice here. **Alis-son's** (207–967–4841) is another place that locals frequent. You might also want to investigate **The Green Heron** (207–967–3315) and the **Satellite Grill** (207–967–0202).

Lodging in Kennebunkport is one of the area's strong drawing points. The facilities are not typical roadside motels. They are historic hotels and inns, and there is a style to suit any tourist. The popularity of this area can make finding a place to stay for the night a challenge, however, even with the large inventory of rooms offered. The following list highlights only a small fraction of those accommodations you might try.

The Nonantum (95 Ocean Avenue; 800–552–5651) is located on the banks of the Kennebunk River and within walking distance to beaches, shops, and art galleries. Rates range from $99 to $199. Children are welcome. **The Kennebunkport Inn** (One Dock Square; 800–248–2621) commands a stately appearance on Dock Square. Rates range from $80 to $200. Children are welcome. **Cabot Cove Cottages** (7 South Main Street; 800–962–5424) are located on a tidal cove of the Kennebunk River, close to beaches and Dock Square.

If you're traveling with pets and looking for something a little more out of the way, try **Four Acres** (207–967–2735), where you can rent cottages near **Goose Rocks Beach.** Other accommodations in the area include the **Yachtsman Motel and Marina** (121 Ocean Avenue; 207–967–2511), **Village Cove Inn** (29 South Maine Street; 800–879–5778), **The Schooners** (Ocean Avenue; 207–967–5333), and the **Rhumb Line Motor Lodge** (Ocean Avenue; 800–337–4862).

SACO

Parents with children will find abundant activities in and around **Saco.** Just 16 miles south of Portland, Saco is a terrific place to call home for a day or two. You will be in easy driving distance of a number of attractions.

With a population of 15,181 people, Saco is not a town that you will feel crowded in, although summer travelers do expand the population considerably. Interstate 95 is the fastest way to reach Saco, but U.S. Route 1 is a more enjoyable path to this summer playground.

Saco and its sister city Biddeford are the heart of York County. If you happen to be in town on the fourth weekend in June, you can attend the annual **Saco Arts Festival** and the **Biddeford LaKermesse Festival.** This four-day extravaganza of parades, food, music, and special events celebrates the area's strong French-Canadian heritage. Whenever you come to town, you can feel sure that there will be plenty to do. The convenient location of Saco puts you in perfect position to visit surrounding sights as well as enjoy the activities right in Saco.

If you and your family are nature lovers, you should put **Saco Heath** on your itinerary. You will find this unusual vacation spot just off the Buxton Road. Five hundred acres of lush grasses, sedge, and reeds make up the heath. In technical terms, the heath is a coalesced domed peatland. It is said that the area was made up of shallow ponds with clay bottoms some

12,000 years ago. As layers of reeds and sphagnum mosses have grown in the local depressions, a spongy dome has been created.

Local groups are working on a boardwalk, and close to half a mile of it should be completed soon. Signs have been erected to explain various types of vegetation and the ecosystem. Some of the plants on the heath are: pitcher plants, sundews, mountain laurel, huckleberry clusters, white cedar, and even cotton grass, which is an arctic species. This is a perfect place for inquisitive children. Parking is not a problem at the heath, and a trail allows access to the natural region. Hours of operation are dawn to dusk. There is no charge for admission. If you would like more information, call the Nature Conservancy at (207) 729–5181.

Aquaboggan may sound a little funny when pronounced, but it's synonymous with children. Kids of all ages, even those of us who are seeing the other side of the hill, can have a blast on a warm day in this fun-park in Saco. What can you and your family do at Aquaboggan? It might take less room to list what you can't do. To make this easy, let's run down the list individually.

Toddlers can frolic in their own splash-and-play section of the park. They can splash around in kiddie pools or slide down kiddie slides. Float tubes are allowed in the water, but big kids aren't. Your youngsters will be playing in the company of their peers, but it is your responsibility to supervise your children. No lifeguards are on duty.

Totally Tubular is the name of an activity that two people can enjoy at once. Mount an inflated tube and ride down the slide. You'll make a big splash at the end, but what could be more refreshing and fun on a hot summer day? Water slides are abundant in this amusement facility, and you can go down on tubes or on the seat of your shorts.

The Aquasaucer is designed for children sixteen years old or younger. Children use ropes to climb the giant, bouncy surface of the Aquasaucer. A spewing fountain of water maintains a slippery surface. Once the pinnacle is claimed, the successful climbers slide to the bottom and splash down into a pool of water that is about 3 feet deep. It's common for two lifeguards to monitor activities on this attraction. Due to the mass appeal of the Aquasaucer, time limits may be enforced to ensure that everyone gets a chance to enjoy the fun.

If you and your children like playing in waves but don't enjoy the salt water of the ocean, visit the wave pool. Mechanically produced waves allow you and your older children to enjoy the simulated action waves in a fun, safe environment. Regular swimming pools also dot the landscape at Aquaboggan.

Aquaboggan also offers dry activities for cloudy, cool days and for those who like their water in glasses. Kiddie and adult bumper boats allow family members to bounce around and into each other's vessel. Skid cars provide the same type of fun on dry land. If driving a Grand Prix race car is a dream of yours, you can do it in a miniaturized version at the park.

Golf aficionados will enjoy the miniature golf course. Shuffle on over to the shuffleboard court and rack up some points to digest the food you find at the snack bar or the ice cream parlor. A gift shop is open to souvenir shoppers, and lockers are provided to customers who wish to store their change of clothes and other articles.

You can bring your own food to the parks's picnic grounds, but leave your grill in the car. Fires are not allowed. Lounge chairs are available, and the park is wheelchair accessible. A first-aid station is on the premises, in the unlikely event someone is injured.

How much does all this fun cost? Several admission options are provided. A Super Ticket costs $23.95 per adult and opens the doors to a majority of the activities. Senior tickets cost $16.95, and Junior tickets are $11.95 for the same privileges. A Pool ticket includes the use of a swimming pool, the wave pool, nine shuffleboard courts, the toddler's splash-and-play area, and one round of mini-golf; it costs $10.50 per person. Group discounts are available, and individual tickets can be purchased for specific activities. Credit cards are welcome, and parking is free and plentiful.

Aquaboggan opens on June 24 and operates from 10:00 A.M. to 6:00 P.M., weather permitting. Labor Day is the last day for fun in the sun. Call (207) 282-3112 for information. When you're on the road, exit 5 off the Maine Turnpike is what you will be looking for to get to Aquaboggan. Then, exit 2B off 195 North in Scarborough will put you on U.S. Route 1. Go 4 miles, into Saco, and Aquaboggan will be on your left.

Funtown/Splashtown USA (774 Portland Road; 207–284–6231) is reached from Interstate 95 by taking exit 5 to U.S. Route 1, where you will drive north for 1 mile to Saco. Water slides are a main attraction here, and swimming pools appear in all shapes and sizes. Loop-de-loop slides provide a new twist to traditional slides. You can drive miniature race cars, sit with a partner and swing yourself around with the power of a massive water hose, or just putt about on the miniature golf course. Young children will get plenty of exercise in the Noah Zark playground. Picnic spots are available.

Also here you will find **Thunder Falls,** the longest, tallest log flume ride in all of New England. Kiddie rides include a merry-go-round, an umbrella ride, swings, helicopters, a Ferris wheel, a Red Baron ride, a kiddie train, and kiddie bumper boats. Rides for older people include, in addition to the log flume, a Tilt-A-Wheel, an antique car ride, a casino, bumper cars, a roller coaster, and an Astrosphere. It's not over yet—there's also a Sea Dragon, a Thunderbolt, a Flying Trapeze, a tea cup ride, Grand Prix race cars, bumper boats, a carousel, and a balloon race. A shooting gallery, an arcade, a gift shop, all sorts of eating places, and other surprises await you. This is one place you should definitely look into. It can provide hours upon hours of fun for people of all ages.

Opening annually in May, the park operates daily from 10:00 A.M. Closing times vary. Like many of the water attractions in Maine, this one closes for the winter, after Labor Day. Parking is free, major credit cards are welcome, and all-day passes or individual tickets may be purchased at varying rates. Call the park for further information on rates and hours.

Especially on rainy or hot days, you'll appreciate a visit to the indoor wonders of the **Maine Aquarium** on U.S. Route 1 in Saco. Like the other nearby parks, it's just 10 miles south of Portland, 2 miles west of Old Orchard Beach, and 12 miles north of Kennebunkport. The aquarium is not particularly large, but it is fascinating. You can see exhibits of live species such as sharks, penguins, eels, lobsters, fish, seals, and other marine creatures. A 30,000-gallon tank holds lemon, sand-tiger, and nurse sharks. You might not expect to find tropical birds at an aquarium, but you'll see them at this one. Venomous fish, such as a lionfish, swim in the aquarium's tanks. The brook trout exhibit takes center stage for fly-fishermen, and multicolored lobsters brighten up other display tanks. Don't miss Old Ralph, as I call him—he's a lobster who weighs maybe thirty-five pounds.

Moray and electric eels glide around, and red-bellied piranhas rule their own tank. Other reptiles and fish fill up the rest of the space in this educational facility—more than 300 varieties of creatures from around the world inhabit this enchanted place.

Many live demonstrations are given. Children love to touch the living specimens of the Tidepool Animal exhibit. A petting zoo is open during the summer, and a duck pond adds to the outside excitement. Harbor seals are on hand for two shows daily. Magellanic penguins pose for pictures as they are fed twice a day. You owe it to yourself and your children to walk through this wonderful aquarium before you leave Maine.

A gift shop and cafe will take care of your desire for souvenirs and light meals. In summertime, you might want to partake of the daily lobster bake.

The aquarium is open daily year-round from 9:00 A.M. to 5:00 P.M.. If you are traveling north on Interstate 95, take exit 5, which is the Saco exit. Go through the tollbooth and take exit 2B to U.S. Route 1, north. Drive 1 mile and look for the aquarium on the right. Parking is free, as is the use of outside picnic tables.

Admission is $6.50 per adult, $5.00 for seniors, $4.50 for ages five through twelve, $2.50 for ages two through four. Major credit cards are accepted. All of the facility is accessible by wheelchair, and air conditioning maintains a comfortable temperature for summer visitors. To get recorded aquarium information dial (207) 284–4511; to reach the business office, call (207) 284–4512.

The remainder of activities in Saco includes many attractions you can enjoy even with only an hour or two to spare. At the **Cascade Golf Range** (207–282–3524) you can drive a bucket of balls or putt for holes-in-one on the miniature golf course. The facility is located on U.S. Route 1 in Saco. If you're up for a full golf game, check out the **Biddeford-Saco Country Club** (207–282–9892) on Old Orchard Road in Saco. You'll find eighteen holes of lush course here.

If golfing is not your interest, try bowling a few games at **Vacationland Bowling and Recreation Center.** Also on U.S. Route 1 in Saco, this establishment offers thirty-two lanes of candlepin bowling, bumper bowling, and billiards. Call (207) 284–7386 for more details.

Maybe you would enjoy a visit to the **York Institute Museum** on

U.S. Route 1 in downtown Saco. A walk through the building will expose you to collections of regional paintings, furnishings, ceramics, glass, and silver. You can call the museum at either (207) 282–3031 or (207) 283–3861. The museum is open 10:00 A.M. to 5:00 P.M. daily.

If the sun is shining and a day on the water sounds good to you, take advantage of local sailing opportunities. **Saco Bay Sailing** (14 Beach Avenue; 207–283–1624) will set you up with a boating experience to remember for years to come. Another sailing opportunity can be found on *Threshold,* at **Camp Ellis Beach.** You can go out for half-day or full-day voyages on a 35-foot wooden ketch. Call (207) 283–4007 for rates and other details.

Saddle up for some fun at **Whistlin' Willows Farm.** A visit to 52 McKenny Road will put you in touch with your equestrian interests. This is a great place to take in Maine's natural beauty on structured trail rides. Call (207) 282–1146 for complete information. The **Bush Brook Stables** (463 West Street in Biddeford; 207–284–7721) also offers trail rides and hayrides.

You're either going to drop from exhaustion in Saco or plan to stay a few days to enjoy it all at your leisure. In either case, you'll need a place to stay. **The Exit 5 Motel and Cottages** at 18 Ocean Park Road will accept your reservations at (207) 284–4727 or (800) 905–4727. **The Saco Motel** at 473 Main Street can be reached at (207) 284–6952 for rates and room availability. **Vacationland Motor Court** on U.S. Route 1 will give you information at (207) 284–6643.

After you have secured a place to stay for the evening, food may be on your mind. What traveler doesn't enjoy a good meal? Well, you can try the menus at **Cornforth House Restaurant** (893 Portland Road; 207–284–2006) or **Kerrymen Pub** (512 Main Street; 207–282–7425). You might also try the fare at **Wormwood's Restaurant,** a fine food establishment at 16 Bay Avenue in Camp Ellis Beach; call (207) 282–9679.

OLD ORCHARD BEACH

Old Orchard Beach is 12 miles south of Portland. You can reach it from Interstate 95 or U.S. Routes 1, 9, or 98. A small town, with a population of only 7,789, Old Orchard Beach caters to tourists. Canadians flock to this resort area, as do people from all parts of the United States. The beach runs for 7 miles and hosts a large pier, which houses dozens of shops, stores, restaurants, and similar establishments. Spending the night at Old Orchard Beach can be done in a campground, a motel, a hotel, a bed and breakfast inn, or even a condominium.

A special treat on this beach is the low surf, which welcomes swimmers. The pier, which has been a fixture of the beach since 1898, was 1,800 feet long at the time of its construction. Big bands once played at a casino on the pier, but a fire and several storms ravaged the long walk out over the ocean. Today's pier is 475 feet long, and the casino is gone. As you move about the streets and shops in Old Orchard Beach, you are as likely to hear French being spoken as you are to hear English. Both languages are common in this fun-filled slice of Maine.

Palace Playland is on the beach at Old Orchard Beach. It features fourteen exciting rides for adults and older children, as well as plenty for youngsters to do. Rain or shine, the Palace Playland is bulging with fun for all. A magnet for children is the giant pinball and video arcade. If you're into history, you might enjoy riding the hand-carved carousel that was made in 1906. For those who are looking to rise to new challenges, take a slide down the largest water slide in all of New England while visiting the Palace Playland. For complete information on this entertaining hot spot, call (207) 934-2001.

While you are exploring the abundant recreational opportunities in Old Orchard Beach, stop by the **Dream Machine** (207-934-0556). It's right on the square and provides electronic games, skeeball, basketball, video games, prizes, and more. **Pirate's Cove Adventure Golf** (207-934-5086) is a championship, thirty-six-hole miniature golf course. It can be found on First Street in Old Orchard Beach.

The Village Park Family Entertainment Center (207-934-7666) is in the shadow of the pier. Here you can practice batting for softball or baseball, play a variety of games, and take in a round of minigolf. **Old Orchard Beach Country Club** is located at 49 Ross Road. This nine-hole course has plenty of beautiful scenery. Call (207) 934-4513 for tee times.

There are so many places to stay in Old Orchard Beach that you would have to spend many vacations there to take them all in. Among the multitude of affordable motels good for families are the **Skylark Motel** (8 Brown Street; 207–934–4235), **The Normandie Motor Inn** (1 York Street; 207–934–2533), **The Ocean House** (70 West Surf Street; 207–934–2847), and **Old Colonial Motel** (61 West Grand Avenue; 888–225–5989).

Grander accommodations can be found at the **Ocean Walk Hotel** (195 East Grand Avenue; 207–934–1716) and the **Grand Beach Inn** (198 East Grand Avenue; 800–926–3242;). If you want a bed and breakfast, try **The Carriage House** (24 Portland Avenue; 207–934–2141). Looking for a place to camp? **Paradise Park** may be just the ticket. This campground is at the top of Main Street and Adelaide Road. Call (207) 934–4633 for reservations and details. If your idea of camping requires a cabin, take a look at **Brookside Cabins** (48 Portland Avenue; 207–934–4753). Its two-bedroom cabins have kitchenettes and screened porches.

Maybe you don't want to cook while vacationing. This is not a problem —Old Orchard Beach is chock-full of restaurants. If you want to enjoy some seafood, consider having dinner at **Joseph's By The Sea** (207–934–5044). This four-star restaurant is located at 55 West Grand Avenue and is known for its creative seafood dishes. Since **Camp Ellis,** a 2000-foot sandy beach on Route 9 in Saco, will probably be on your list of destinations when you are touring the Old Orchard Beach area, treat yourself to some fine seafood at **Braley's Restaurant** (207–282–5842) on Maine Avenue in Camp Ellis. Braley's offers lobster and steamers, among other entrees.

How do blueberry pancakes sound for breakfast? If your mouth is watering for some down-home cooking that will make your morning special, take a ride to **Barefoot Boy Restaurant** (45 East Grand Avenue; 207–934–9587). Opening at 7:00 A.M. and keeping the fires burning until everyone clears out, this restaurant serves breakfast, lunch, and dinner.

Feel like a little ice cream? **Captain Maxie's** at 11 Bay Avenue in Camp Ellis Beach can fix you up with twenty-eight flavors and fifteen toppings. There's more on the menu here, too. Sit on the waterfront and enjoy everything from salads to fried foods and lobster. The adults might like to indulge in some gourmet coffee. You can call this beachside restaurant at (207) 284–5275.

SCARBOROUGH

The town of **Scarborough** is just north of Old Orchard Beach, where Route 207 (Black Point Road) meets Route 77. The great American painter Winslow Homer called this part of Maine home. Within the 49 square miles known as Scarborough, the communities of Scarborough, **Pine Point,** and **Prouts Neck** can be found. More than 12,500 people live in this region, with Prouts Neck being known for its exclusive homes.

Pine Point provides a beach, accommodations, sportfishing, and restaurants. Prouts Neck claims the oldest home in the area—the **Hunniwell House,** built in 1673. You can tour this home during the summer months, but an appointment must be made in advance. The house is located at 83 Black Point Road. Admission is free. Call (207) 883–8427 for information. Beaches include **Prouts Neck, Pine Point Beach, Higgins Beach, Scarborough Beach,** and **Western Beach.** Parking is not a problem for most of these beaches under normal tourist activity periods.

Scarborough Marsh is Maine's largest salt marsh, and it is home to a **Maine Audubon Society nature center** (207–883–5100) on Route 9, east of Route 1. Starting in mid-June, visitors can rent canoes and explore the site's 3,100 acres of marsh and river. A detailed map that helps identify exceptional plants, birds, and animals is offered to explorers. Hours of operation are from 9:30 A.M. to 5:30 P.M.

Scarborough Downs (207–883–4331) is off exit 6 of Interstate 95 (also known in this section as the Maine Turnpike). Take exit 6, pass through the tollbooth, turn left on Payne Road, and drive for one quarter of a mile, then turn right at the racetrack entrance. You and your family can dine in the **Downs Club Restaurant** while enjoying harness racing at its finest. The dining room is directly across from the finish line, and each table has its own television monitor for close-up viewing of the horses and sulkies. Mutuel windows are close by for your convenience in making wagers.

If you prefer riding horses to watching horses, **Longhorn Equestrian Center** (207–883–1600 or 800–883–6499; 338 Broadturn Street) offers guided trail rides for adults, as well as kiddie and pony rides. If it's winter and the horses are cold, turn your attention to **Beech Ridge Farm Cross Country Ski Center** (207–839–4098; 193 Beech Ridge Road). Here you will find 150 acres of fields and woods to explore on your skis.

A warming hut is available for everyone and is especially useful for younger children. You can rent equipment and get lessons at this facility. The Center is open 9:00 A.M. to dusk, but it's best to call first.

PORTLAND

The **Children's Museum of Maine** should be one of your first stops in this old port town. Located at 746 Stevens Avenue, the museum (207–828–1234) is open daily from 9:30 A.M. to 4:30 P.M. This is not some boring building that your kids will have to be dragged through. In fact, you will probably have trouble keeping up with your children in this fun-filled learning center. What can you expect to find?

One section of the building is set aside for toddlers only. They can slide down a small slide, play peek-a-boo from a plastic fort, or be fascinated by carnival-type mirrors. This is a small area of the facility, but it is a safe haven for little tykes.

Other areas offer fascinating activities in many subjects of interest. Let your children stick their heads into the center of an ant colony, for instance. A large ant farm is on display with provisions for children to rise up among the ants, protected by plexiglass, for a close-up view. In another area, energetic kids can scale a spider's web (a rope climbing net). A trip down on the farm will allow your kids to milk a plastic cow and see other farm items.

Finding a food basket at the grocery store here can be difficult. Children love to assume roles as cashiers while their peers collect plastic groceries. Just outside the grocery store is a boat that rocks to and fro on a wood platform. Kids get to use an automatic teller machine to learn the mechanics of money. If your family is into spelunking, you will enjoy the cave tunnel that you can walk through. A fire truck is always filled with children, and we haven't left the first floor yet.

A spaceship awaits your children on the second floor. Ride the stationary bike and watch the skeleton in front of you demonstrate how your bones are moving. A huge globe of the world rotates on a base and allows children to turn it until their arms get tired. Balls hovering over a shaft of air captivates children; other exhibits are equally fun. There is a lot to do, and most of it adds to the learning experience that children need.

A gift shop is located on the first floor. Parents enjoy taking breaks in the vending-machine cafe, downstairs. Special activities that kids enjoy are offered on a regular basis. With an admission cost of only $2.50, this is a lot of affordable family fun at any time of the year.

For a bird's eye view of the city talk to the folks at **Hot Fun.** They offer hot-air balloon rides with up to six passengers allowed. Call (207) 799–0193 for current details on ballooning over Casco Bay.

Finding culture in Portland is not a problem. The **Portland Museum of Art** (207–775–6148) at 7 Congress Square is Maine's largest art museum. It has an extensive collection of American artists. You will also see the work of Renoir, Degas, and Picasso on display. Hours of operation are Tuesday, Wednesday, and Saturday 10:00 A.M. to 5:00 P.M., Thursday and Friday 10:00 A.M. to 9:00 P.M., and Sunday from noon until 5:00 P.M. Fees for adults are $6.00; senior citizens and students with I.D. are charged $5.00; children six to twelve get in for $1.00, and children under six get in free. Admission is free for everyone on Friday from 5:00 to 9:00 P.M.

Railroad enthusiasts will enjoy a stop at the **Maine Narrow-Gauge Railroad Co. & Museum** (207–828–0814). A collection of narrow-gauge rail equipment has been assembled at 58 Fore Street. You can get in daily from 10:00 A.M. to 4:00 P.M. Admission to the museum is free. Kids of all ages will be pleased by the small rail cars that saw regular use from the 1870s to the 1940s. Among the collection is a two-foot parlor car said to be the only one in the world, Rangeley locomotives, a railbus, and a Model-T inspection car. Once you have seen all you want to see, hop aboard one of the running trains for a ride of about 2 miles. A ticket will cost adults $5.00, senior citizens sixty-two and older $4.00, and children between four and twelve $3.00. Children under four get in free. Rides are given on weekends only until about the middle of May. If you like trains, this depot is for you.

Lighthouses are the subject of the museum at the **Museum at Portland Head Light** (207–799–2661). This museum is open June through October from 10:00 A.M. to 4:00 P.M. The site can be visited in November, December, April, and May on weekends from 10:00 A.M. to 4:00 P.M. Located at 1000 Shore Road in **Fort Williams Park,** this is the oldest lighthouse in Maine. It was brought into service in 1791 under the order of

George Washington. Kids will enjoy the endless view and learning about the interesting facets of life in a lighthouse. To get to Fort Williams Park, leave Portland on State Street (Route 77) and head south until you enter **South Portland.** Take a left turn on Broadway and a right on Cottage Street, which will turn into Shore Road.

If seeing all the beautiful water makes you want to go for a cruise, you can do so easily. Islands dot **Casco Bay** and invite visitors to their shores. **Long Island** has a general store and a restaurant. **Great Chebeague** is home to a classic summer hotel. **Peaks Island** is another great place to visit. Families can rent bikes at **Peaks Island Mercantile** (207–766–5631) or learn to paddle a sea kayak at **Maine Island Kayak Co.** (207–766–2373). A meal at **Will's** on Peaks Island allows you to enjoy a beautiful view of Portland. **Great Diamond Island** offers food and lodging. **Cliff Island** is a long ride (about 1 1/2 hours) but you are greeted with sandy beaches once you arrive. The cottages, wildflowers, and quiet inlets of the various islands are inviting. How can you get out there to enjoy them? Take a ferry from one of the many companies offering service to the islands.

Casco Bay Lines (207–774–7871) at the Casco Bay Ferry Terminal at 56 Commercial Street can get you to any of the islands. Rates vary depending on where you are going. If you want to ride the daily mail boat, you will be out for close to three hours at a cost of $9.50 per adult, $8.00 for seniors, and $4.25 per child. Children under five ride free. The boat puts in at all the islands in the morning and again in the afternoon. Other seasonal cruises are offered by **Eagle Tours, Inc.** (207–774–6498) and **Bay View Cruises** (207–761–0496).

Looking for a place to eat and rest for the night? Don't worry. Food and lodging is so abundant in Portland that a complete book could be written on the subject. One claim states that Portland has more restaurants per capita than any other city in America. It is also said that there are more than 2,000 hotel and motel rooms in and around Portland. Lodging ranges from the inexpensive traveler chains to elegant inns and hotels. The **Holiday Inn by the Bay** (207–775–2311) offers affordable arrangements for families at their 88 Spring Street location. The **Pomegranate Inn** (207–772–1006) at 49

ROGER'S FAVORITE ANNUAL EVENTS IN SOUTHERN MAINE

York Summerfest, York; 207–363–4422
Strawberry Festival, South Berwick; 207–439–1319
York Days Celebration, York; 207–363–4422
Harvest Fest, York; 207–363–4422
Big Patriot's Day Celebration, Ogunquit Beach; 207–646–2939
Wells Week, Wells; 207–646–2451
Sand Building Contest, Ogunquit Beach; 207–646–2939
Nature Crafts Festival, Laudholm Farm; 207–646–2451
Christmas Parade, Wells; 207–646–2451
Harbor Park Day, Wells; 207–646–2451

Neal Street is a pleasant diversion from interstate motel chains. Its room prices range from $95 to $150 a night.

Sleeping on the islands can be expensive, but it is a wonderful experience. Try the **Chebeague Inn By-the-Sea** (207–864–5155) on Chebeague Island. You and the kids can swim at **Hamilton Beach,** play a round of golf on a public course below the hotel, or go exploring on bikes. If it rains, snuggle in next to the massive stone fireplace and play a variety of board games. The price of a double room runs from $70 to $130. **Keller's** (207–766–2441) on Peaks Island is open year-round and is close to the ferry landing. This guest house used to be a general store and restaurant. A beach is on the property, and a double room rents for $75. Credit cards are not accepted, but personal checks are.

Finding good food in Portland is never a problem. A favorite place for families as well as business professionals is **DiMillo's Floating Restaurant** (207–772–2216) at Long Wharf. Open for lunch and dinner, this restaurant is Maine's only floating eatery. Menu items include seafood, steak, Italian cuisine, and little meals for children. Entrees start at less than $10.00. The water views from this restaurant are wonderful. They're open from 11:00 A.M. to 11:00 P.M.

The Porthole (207–774–3448) at 32 Customs Wharf is open early for breakfast and serves lunch and dinner at family prices. An all-you-can-eat fish fry at lunch is only $3.95. The accommodations aren't fancy, but the food is good and inexpensive. If pizza is more to your liking, try **Anthony's Italian Kitchen** (207–774–8668) at 151 Middle Street. Pizza lovers will agree that it doesn't get any better than this. Burgers, burgers, and more burgers are what you will find at **Ruby's Choice** (127 Commercial Street; 207–773–9099). This is a great, affordable place to take the kids.

FREEPORT

Put on the map by the presence of L. L. Bean's store, Freeport draws thousands of visitors each day. L. L. Bean's is surely one of the main attractions in Freeport, but it is far from the only one. Outlet stores for shoes, clothes, skis, and other items are plentiful in Freeport, as are gift shops, restaurants, hot dog stands, ice cream parlors, and inns. Another big pull to this area is the **Desert of Maine.** Allow plenty of time for your visit to Freeport, and bring some good walking shoes.

Family campers can stay at the **Desert of Maine Campground** (207–865–6962) at 95 Desert Road, not far from the action in downtown Freeport. Take Route 1 south from the center of town (1 mile) and take a right onto Desert Road. Campground is at the end, directly across from the desert. Campsites cost $15 to $18 per night and include hook-ups, hot showers, laundry facilities, a convenience store, propane, fire rings, picnic tables, horseshoe pits, and nature trails. The biggest attraction, however, is the desert itself. A gift shop is also available.

Few people would expect to find a desert in Maine, but this one is for real—it's even been featured on Ripley's *Believe It or Not* television show. Geologists have determined that a glacier slid through the area some 8,000 years ago and began to create the desert. This desert is open to visitors daily from mid-May to mid-October from 9:00 A.M. to dusk. Entrance fees for adults is $4.75 and $2.75 for children. Senior citizens get in for $4.25. Narrated coach tours are included in the price and provide a good explanation of the formation of the desert.

If you and your family want to venture off on your own, go right ahead. There's about forty acres of sand to see that was once farmland. The Tuttle Farm, as the desert was once known, was heavily farmed and then logged off to feed the railroad's need for timber. In the process, glacial sand deposits began to rise. They now cover old farm buildings and trees. It's an amazing sight. The sand is rich in mineral deposits that make it unstable for commercial use, but local rockhounds love it, as do children.

When you come back from your tour of the desert, check out the 1783 barn that is full of exhibits. Your kids can see old farm implements and push buttons to put displays into motion. Another good attraction is the sand-art area. Kids can make their own sand art or watch other artists at work. You can even buy colored sand to take home with you. The desert is less than 3 miles from the hub of Freeport.

L. L. Bean (95 Main Street; 800–341–4341, ext 7801 or 207–865–4761) is a store, but it's much more. This landmark is a Maine tradition, and there's plenty under its roof to keep your kids busy while you shop. Children can marvel at the live trout swimming in the indoor pool or contemplate the porcupine and bears (both stuffed) that stand guard around the camping section. Taxidermists have created a virtual wildlife show throughout this store with moose heads, bears, foxes, ducks, birds, fish, and other animals represented.

Some kids just enjoying riding the elevator between floors. Others are fascinated by the on-screen demonstrations that are given in various departments on everything from canoeing to turkey hunting. If you think that L. L. Bean is only for people who enjoy hunting, fishing, and camping, you're wrong. These areas are covered nicely, but other attractions include clothes, lots of clothes, travel bags, housewares, books, dog accessories, footwear, canoes, and so forth. If you have any interest in outdoor activities, L. L. Bean probably has what you are looking for, and the store is open twenty-four hours a day.

Parking is free at Bean's. If you're hot when you arrive, stop into **Ben & Jerry's** ice cream shop. The prices are a little steep, but the ice cream is delicious. You won't have any trouble finding a street vendor around Bean's who will sell you some good hot dogs. Once you have parked in Bean's lot, you can explore most of Freeport on foot. Many parking lots are available for vehicles of all sizes, but you will have to walk awhile, so come prepared.

Shopping is very big business in Freeport. At last count, there were more than 125 outlet stores. According to one report, L. L. Bean is said to attract about 2.5 million customers each year. When you consider that this number of people is probably twice the total population of Maine, there is no wonder why Freeport seems crazy in the tourist season. You can buy anything from herbs to brass to buttons in Freeport. Only a handful of the shops concentrate on items of interest to children, so you may have to split parental duties for shopping and entertaining. Kids can be kept busy at many locations ranging from restaurants to shops, but their patience may run out before you peruse all of the buying opportunities for adults. For more information call (207) 865–1713.

If you have deep pockets and would like to see Freeport from the air, you can contact **Freeport Balloon Company** at (207) 865–1712. They offer year-round hot-air balloon rides at $150 per person, with a maximum of three passengers, not counting the pilot. Rides last about one hour. Reservations and a deposit are required.

A more down-to-earth experience might be canoeing. The **Harraseeket River** is popular with local canoers. The trips normally start at **Mast Landing,** but other launch sites are available at **Winslow Memorial Park** on Staples Point Road and at **South Freeport Harbor.** The **Maine Audubon Society** (207–781–2330) gives periodic, scheduled guided trips. *The Atlantic Seal* (207–865–6112) offers three-hour cruises to **Eagle Island,** the former summer home of Admiral Robert E. Peary, the first man to reach the North Pole. Seals and osprey are the subject of summer trips; foliage is the main interest of fall excursions. Lobstering demonstrations are usually included on these cruises, except on Sundays, when lobstering is prohibited.

The local parks can add to your Freeport adventure. **Winslow Memorial Park** (207–865–4198) on Staples Point Road is open Memorial Day through September. This ninety-acre municipal park has a sandy beach and a large, grassy picnic area. Boating and camping is also available, as are rest rooms and showers. **Wolfe's Neck Woods State Park** (207–865–4465) is open from Memorial Day to Labor Day. This 244-acre park offers opportunities for shoreline hiking along Casco Bay, the Harraseeket River, and salt marshes. Also nearby is **Mast Landing Sanctuary.** Maintained by the Maine Audubon Society, this 100-acre area has trails through apple orchards, woods, meadows, and along a mill stream.

When you're ready for a rest, you'll find many inns and bed & breakfasts in Freeport. One of the most popular, but expensive, places to stay and dine is the **Harraseeket Inn** (207–865–9377). This luxury hotel is just two blocks from L. L. Bean and the main shopping area of downtown Freeport. Antiques, canopy beds, and whirlpool tubs are all found in this charming setting. A drawing room, a library, a ballroom, a formal dining room, and an informal tavern are part of its appeal. Rates run from $145 to $225.

The **White Cedar Inn** (207–865–9099) at 178 Main Street was once home to Donald B. MacMillian, who accompanied Admiral Peary to the North Pole. Rates here begin at $80 a night. The **Holbrook Inn** (207–865–6693) at 7 Holbrook Street has queen-size beds, private baths, air conditioning, and antique furnishings. Double rooms are $75.00. If you decide to go a little south of Freeport, you can find modern motels, such as the **Freeport Inn** (800–99–VALUE or 207–865–3106), where prices are lower.

Once you have a place to stay, you may want to eat. A full smorgasbord of dining delights is available to you in the Freeport Area. Fast-food chain restaurants are apparent along Main Street but maybe you want a meal you haven't had in dozens of other places. Try something new. **The Blue Onion** (207–865–9396) on Route 1 at the southern end of town offers good food for a fair price. You can get anything from lobster to soup at this indoor-outdoor eatery that is happy to have your children as guests. Seafood lovers enjoy the **Muddy Rudder** (207–846–3082) on Route 1 south of Freeport. This is a fine family atmosphere where prices are not outrageous. The **China Rose** (207–865–6886) at 10 School Street offers Szechuan-Mandarin and Hunan food at reasonable rates. **Crickets Restaurant** (207–865–4005) at 175 Lower Main Street is popular with the locals for its wide variety of menu items for breakfast, lunch, and dinner, at family prices.

As you make your way through southern Maine, there will be no shortage of attractions and activities. If anything, you will run out of time before you run out of ideas for adventure. Save some of your vacation for the rest of the state, however—there is much to do along the roads in front of you.

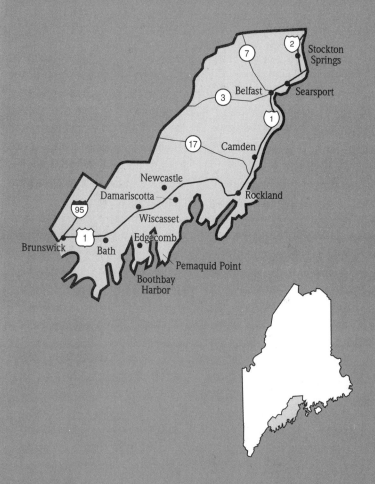

Mid-Coast Maine

Mid-Coast Maine

The Mid-Coast region of Maine is full of fun. There are islands that you can visit by car, lighthouses to see, and plenty of good restaurants in which to savor the taste of Maine. You can drive around the edges of the coast and see working fishing villages, visit historical sites, or spend a few days on any of the numerous beaches along this stretch of Maine. Whether you are swimming at Coffin Pond in Brunswick, searching the tidal pools at Reid State Park, or checking out the ships in Boothbay Harbor, you and your children are sure to enjoy your time as you work your way up the coast of Maine.

BRUNSWICK

As you travel north out of Freeport on either Route 1 or Interstate 95, you'll arrive next in **Brunswick,** a charming town that is home to **Bowdoin College** and the **Brunswick Naval Air Station.** Brunswick provides access to Topsham, Bath, Harpswell, Orr's Island, and Bailey Island. It is a local profit center for many businesses and provides visitors with diverse entertainment options.

You might begin a tour of Brunswick at **Bowdoin College** (207–725–3000) on Maine Street. Its Maine State Music Theater offers many theatrical shows throughout the year. The **Bowdoin College Museum of Art** (Upper Park Road, Walker Art Building; 207–725–3275) houses outstanding art collections and offers various special exhibits.

The **Peary–MacMillian Arctic Museum** (Hubbard Hall; 207–725–3000), also at Bowdoin, displays clothing, trophies, and other mementos from expeditions to the North Pole by Robert Edwin Peary (class of 1877) and Donald Baxter MacMillian (class of 1898). Hours for both museums are 10:00 A.M. to 5:00 P.M. Tuesday through Saturday and 2:00 to 5:00 P.M. Sunday. There is no fee, but donations are accepted. The college covers 110 acres and includes more than fifty buildings. Tours can be arranged by appointment.

The **Pejepscot Historical Society Museums** (207–729–6606) include three separate sites. A combination pass to all the historical society museums is $5.00 per adult and $2.00 per child. The **Pejepscot Museum** at 159 Park Row is open weekdays from 9:00 A.M. to 4:30 P.M. Additional days are offered during the summer season. Admission to this site alone is free. This facility exhibits materials that show the history of Brunswick, Topsham, and Harpswell. Another site is the **Skolfield–Whittier House** at 161 Park Row. This seventeen-room mid-nineteenth-century home was sealed for fifty years, preserving its original furnishings and decor. Summer tours are given Tuesday through Friday from 10:00 A.M. to 3:00 P.M. and on Saturdays from 1:00 to 4:00 P.M. Admission to this site alone is $4.00 for adult tours; children aged six to twelve are charged $2.00. This is an excellent opportunity for your children to see how people of the past lived.

The third site is the **Joshua L. Chamberlain Museum** at 226 Maine Street. It's open during the summer from Tuesday through Saturday, from 10:00 A.M. to 4:00 P.M. Admission to this site alone is $3.00 per adult and $2.00 per child. Joshua Chamberlain was a college professor who became known for his Civil War heroics on Little Round Top during the Battle of Gettysburg. He also served four terms as the governor of Maine and was the president of Bowdoin College. The museum occupies five restored rooms of Chamberlain's house. Displays include Civil War artifacts and memorabilia of General Chamberlain. Said to be one of Brunswick's most unusual homes, the structure started out as a typical Cape Cod in the mid-1820s. When Chamberlain bought it in 1871, he had the house raised vertically by 11 feet and inserted a new ground floor of living space.

If you are ready for more active adventure, consider taking a dip in one of the local swimming holes. **White's Beach** (207–729–0415) is a campground with a swimming area, a sandy beach, and a small water slide. It's a little out of town, on the Durham Road, and it can be crowded during prime season. Call for rates and hours of operation. **Thomas Point Beach** (207–725–6009) is off Route 24 near the section of town known as Cook's Corner. This is a good picnic spot, and there's lots of room for kids to roam. The sandy beach is on tidal water, so low tide presents swimmers with mud flats. This is a nice place to let kids explore unusual creatures like horseshoe crabs. Sixty-four acres of lawns and groves, a playground for kids, and a snack bar and arcade round out the areas of exploration and entertainment. In addition, special events are staged here throughout the summer season. Admission is $2.50 for adults and $2.00 for children. The area is open daily from Memorial Day to Labor Day from 9:00 A.M. to sunset. Call for information on special events.

   Coffin Pond (207–725–6656) on the River Road just a short ways from Pleasant Street is a fine family spot for swimming. A sandy beach surrounds a town-owned pond/pool where a large water slide has kids standing in line to splash down. Lifeguards are on duty, and the swimming is safe for kids of all ages with reasonable supervision. Picnic tables are scattered among trees, and a playground is open to children. The food from the snack bar is good and not as expensive as you might expect. Call for hours of operation and fees. The fees are minimal, but they do change.

   A **Fishway Viewing** area, located on the Androscoggin River and Maine Street at the **Brunswick-Topsham Hydro Station** is a fun, free place to take kids in May and June. A fish ladder allows fish to migrate over the dam in the river. As the fish, like salmon, move upriver, they pass the counting and viewing area for all to see. Hours of operation are Saturday and Sunday from 10:00 A.M. to 2:00 P.M. and Wednesday from 7:00 P.M. to 9:00 P.M.

   If your children enjoy miniature golf or driving a bucket of balls on a range, take a ride up Bath Road, past Cook's Corner, to visit the **Long Shot Golf Center** (207–725–6377) at 305 Bath Road. It's on the left with a large sign. You can't miss the waterfall on the miniature course. If the weather doesn't favor outdoor activities, **Yankee Lanes of Brunswick** (207–725–2963) provides indoor bowling. This large bowling alley is on

ROGER'S FAVORITE ANNUAL EVENTS IN MID-COAST MAINE

Military Aviation and Aerobatic Show, Owls Head;
    207–594–4418
Belfast Bay Festival, Belfast; 207–338–5900
Maine Coast Competition, Belfast; 207–338–2478
Annual Maine Lobster Festival, Rockland; 207–596–0376
Transportation Rally and Aerobatic Spectacular, Owls Head;
    207–594–4418
Maine Coast Artists' Annual State of the Art Auction, Rockport;
    207–236–2875
Members of the New York Philharmonic on Concert, Belfast;
    207–338–1945
Damariscotta River Oyster Festival, Damariscotta; 207–563–8340
Olde Bristol Days, Pemaquid Beach; 207–563–8340

the right side of Bath Road, just before the golf course. **Hoyts Brunswick Cinema Ten** (207–798–3996) at 19 Gurnet Road offers another solution to rainy days. Readers can take a break while in the Cook's Corner area and visit the area's largest bookstore: **Greater Bookland & Cafe** is located in the shopping mall at Cook's Corner.

Cook's Corner provides plenty of fast-food types of places to eat, as well as a toy store called **Toy Works** (207–725–8741). A sub shop, a pizza place, and a **Denny's** family restaurant (10 Gurnet Road; 207–729–0846) are all in sight of each other. Other restaurants in the general area include **Captain Mike's** (207–729–4951) at 32 Bath Road, **The Chuck Wagon** (207–729–9896) at 42 Bath Road, **Ernie's Drive In** (207–729–9439) at 18 Bath Road, and **Fat Boy Drive-In** (207–729–9431) at 111 Bath Road. A little ice cream store is along this same stretch of road. All of these eateries are priced reasonably and provide good food.

Downtown Brunswick, which is only about 2 miles from Cook's Corner, offers food of all types and for all budgets. **The Barking Spider** (207–721–9662) at 94 Maine Street is always a hit with the kids. Burgers, pizza, potato skins, and a variety of other foods fill out the menu with low prices and large portions. **The Great Impasta** (207–729–5858) at 42 Maine Street serves Italian food for lunch and dinner, but the prices can be a little high. **Vincenzo's Restaurant** (207–729–9122) at 15 Cushing Street caters to families; it offers everything from pizza to fried clams. **Amato's** (207–729–5514) at 135 Maine Street is a gathering place for local teenagers; you and your kids can get anything from a sandwich to a meatball sub to a slice of pizza. **Rosita's Mexican Food** (207–729–7118) at 212 Maine Street serves authentic Mexican food at family prices. The **China Pearl** (207–725–8686) at 112 Pleasant Street is a favorite place for Chinese food. The streets of Brunswick are lined with food places that range from **Danny's Dogs** (a hot dog vendor on the local town green) to elegant dining such as the **Captain Daniel Stone Inn** (207–725–9898) at 10 Water Street.

If you're hoping to spend the night in Brunswick, the **Comfort Inn** (207–729–1129) at 199 Pleasant Street is a very nice place to stay, and the prices are fair (from $60 per room in winter to $85 in summer). The **Viking Motor Inn** (207–729–6661) at 287 Bath Road is a small, older facility with moderate rates ($35 to $45 per room). The **Super 8 Motel** (207–725–8883) at 224 Bath Road also offers clean, basic accommodations at fair prices ($42 to $55 per room). If you have your heart set on a pool, try the **Interstate Oasis Econo Lodge** (207–729–9991) or the **Maineline Motel** (207–725–8761), both on Pleasant Street. These two motels don't present the same image as some others do, but they do have outdoor pools. The **Atrium Inn & Convention Center** (207–729–5555) at 21 Gurnet Road at Cook's Corner has a small indoor pool and a health club, but rates can run high. Other options for lodging include the **Captain Daniel Stone Inn** (10 Water Street, Brunswick; 207–725–9898), rates from $99 to $175 per room; the **Brunswick Bed & Breakfast** (165 Park Row, Brunswick; 207–729–4914), rates from $73 to $103 per room; **The Samuel Newman House** (7 South Street, Brunswick; 207–725–3822), rates from $60 to $65 per room; and the **Stowe House** (63 Federal Street, Brunswick; 207–725–5543), rates range from $69 to $79 per room.

Before you leave the Brunswick area, you owe it to yourself and your kids to take a ride down Route 24 to explore Great Island, Orr's Island, and Bailey Island. This is a trip that you should plan to take when the weather is good and you're in no hurry. There are not a lot of commercial attractions on this tour, but the scenery and the salt air will do wonders for you. And, there are enough diversions along the way to keep your kids satisfied.

Start your journey on Route 24 at Cook's Corner. Follow the signs out of town to the islands. The first bridge you cross, just a few miles down the road, puts you on **Great Island.** There's not much to see here except lobster boats and buoys, so just keep going straight on Route 24. If you want a chance to see some seals, turn left shortly after crossing the bridge onto the island, at the Cundy's Harbor Road. There is a sign at the intersection. Stay on this road until you run out of dry land—it won't take very long. You will be in picturesque **Cundy's Harbor** in just a few minutes, where lobstermen will be mending their traps and seals may be swimming playfully or resting on shore. This side trip will give you a taste of how the real Mainers live and work in a harbor area. Once you've run low on film, retrace your path back to Route 24, turn left, and head for Orr's Island.

You'll know that you are on **Orr's Island** when you dip down into a low spot and cross over some of the most beautiful green water you've ever seen. As you reach the top of the hill, there will be a small pull-off with picnic tables on your left. This is a pleasant place to take a break, but keep an eye on your kids. The road is a busy one in season and the back side of the picnic area is steep and leads to deep water.

As you continue along on Route 24, you will see many little side roads worth exploring. Lowell Cove Road, on your left, leads to a small cove, **Lowell Cove,** where a whale came in for a visit a few years ago. This is a good place to stop and let the kids run around on the natural beach. They should wear shoes; this is not a sandy area. Shells and glass may cut bare feet. Once you are back on the road, you will see a number of tourist stops selling everything from art to old buoys.

When you cross from Orr's Island to **Bailey Island,** you will do so on the only remaining **cribstone bridge** in the world. The bridge is made with granite blocks that are laid in a honeycomb pattern, without cement, to allow tidal flows to pass. The bridge is narrow, but sturdy.

On Bailey Island you will see **Mackerel Cove** on your right and down low, filled with a variety of boats. This is a colorful place to take some pictures and to explore the water's edge. There is also a restaurant at the marina, but we'll talk about food and lodging a little later. When you continue down Route 24, you won't have much farther to go. The road will cease at **Land's End,** where a fascinating gift shop, a small beach, and terrific views will capture your attention.

When you begin your return trip, you might be interested in a place to stay for the night or a good restaurant. Both are available on the islands. **Driftwood Inn and Cottages** (Driftwood Road; 207–833–5461) offers lodging on Bailey Island for very reasonable rates ($70 double occupancy). Open from June through mid-October, this facility has been in the same family for over fifty years. Kids will get a kick out of the small saltwater swimming pool that is set into the rocky shore. You and your family can enjoy the dining room from late June through Labor Day. Almost all of the rooms and cottages have views of the ocean, and the personal attention from your hosts will not be forgotten. Other accommodations on the islands include the **Bailey Island Motel** (207–833–2886), **Cook's Island View Motel** (207–833–7780), and **Log Cabin Lodging & Fine Food** (207–833–5546). Other guest houses may be noticed along your route. Stop to inquire if any interest you.

Food on the islands naturally focuses on seafood specialties, but you and your kids can get some land-lover's food if seafood is not your favorite. **Cook's Lobster House** (Garrison Cove Road; 207–833–2818), in sight of the bridge between Orr's and Bailey's Islands, is a good place to eat, but service can be slow due to the large number of customers that this waterfront spot can accommodate. The prices on some dishes can be steep. **Jack Baker's Ocean View Restaurant** (207–833–5366), on the left just after crossing the cribstone bridge onto Bailey Island, puts on a good feed at fair prices. Views are good, and the kids can play around in the rocky tidal pools after eating.

The Original Log Cabin Restaurant (207–833–5546), a little farther down the road on Bailey Island, is competitive in its pricing. Service is usually okay, and the food is good. **Mackerel Cove Restaurant** (207–833–6656) at Mackerel Cove on Bailey Island offers both a coffee shop and a restaurant. This is a working pier, and the language can get pretty salty. If you have impressionable children, this probably isn't a great place to stop for lunch. Otherwise, the service is usually fast and the prices are fair. When you dock back at Cook's Corner, you can turn right and head into Bath.

BATH

Bath is a strategic Maine town due to its proximity to the **Kennebec River.** Some 5,000 vessels have been built in the Bath shipyards. Today, the **Bath Iron Works** (BIW), is the shipbuilder in the area. Popham Colony settlers, downriver from Bath, launched a 30-ton pinnace, the *Virginia,* in 1607, but today, it's American naval ships that you see docked near the drawbridge in Bath. The first feature you are likely to see in Bath is a red-and-white crane that reaches approximately 400 feet into the air at BIW. This is the largest crane on the East Coast. Bath is built around the shipyard, but there is more to this town than just tugboats and welders.

One attraction that may interest your children is the **Maine Maritime Museum** (243 Washington Street; 207–443–1316), which includes the **Percy & Small Shipyard,** the country's only surviving wooden ship-building yard. Most of the exhibits are post–Civil War, when about 80 percent of the country's full-rigged ships were built in Maine. Nearly half of them were built in Bath. If you can believe what you hear, the museum now holds about one million pieces of art, artifacts, and documents. There is something here for everyone to enjoy, and it is worth the time and price of admission.

The museum is open daily, year-round, from 9:30 A.M. to 5:00 P.M. Admission is $7.75 for adults and $5.00 for kids between the ages of six and fifteen, with a maximum family (two adults and two or more children) admission of $22.00. The museum is closed on such holidays as Thanksgiving, Christmas, and New Year's Day.

Bath has your standard fast-food places to eat, but two other places are out of this world for family food. One is in West Bath on the Bath Road. It is the **New Meadows Inn** (207–443–3921) where you can just eat or spend the night in a room or a cottage, all at reasonable prices. Buffets are common at this restaurant, and you and the kids can sit at a water-view window while enjoying an all-you-can-eat meal at down-home prices. A little-known but fabulous place for a quick, delicious lunch is the **Front Street Deli and Club** (207–443–9815). This little hideout is at 128 Front Street. If you enter from the main entrance, you will find booths and a family setting. Go downstairs, and you have ambiance like you wouldn't believe, complete with the club cat who may take a nap on your feet as you sit in overstuffed couches and chairs. Not only is the setting of this place unique, so is the food. A favorite is the chicken-salad BLT. That's right—you get a chicken salad sandwich and a BLT all packed into one double-decker meal. It's great! For interesting food, calm eating conditions, and a setting you won't want to leave, check out the Front Street Deli and Club.

Some other good places to eat include the **Bath House of Pizza** (207–443–6631) at 737 Washington Street, **The Cabin** (207–443–6224) at 552 Washington Street (where great pizza is the meal of the day), the **Harbor Lights Cafe** (207–443–9883) at 166 Front Street, **Truffles Cafe** (207–442–8474) at 21 Elm Street, and **J.R. Maxwell's** (207–443–4461) at 122 Front Street. Many other good restaurants dot the Bath streets.

Overnight accommodations can be arranged at the **Holiday Inn-Bath** (207–443–9741) in plain view of Route 1 as you enter town. It offers a super breakfast menu in the dining room, along with lunches and dinners. Its Bounty Lounge is a nightspot for area residents, and a sauna and hot tub is available to guests. Rates range from $79 to $89 per room. For travelers who prefer inns or bed & breakfast arrangements, consider the **Fairhaven Inn** (207–443–4391) on North Bath Road; the **Inn at Bath** (207–443–4294) at 969 Washington Street, where you can occupy a suite with a sitting room in a former hay loft; the **Packard House** (207–443–6069) at 45 Pearl Street; or **Elizabeth's Bed & Breakfast** (207–443–1146) at 360 Front Street. Rates for the above accommodations range from $50 to $150.

When you leave Bath going north on Route 1, you can either stay on Route 1 and head for **Wiscasset,** known as the "Prettiest Little Village in Maine," or you can turn right at the Dairy Queen just after crossing the drawbridge that spans the Kennebec and head out for some fun in the sun at **Reid State Park,** located on Route 127. **Popham Beach** is another worthy destination to consider *before* crossing the bridge. If you have the time, take a trip to the beaches before continuing north.

Popham Beach State Park (207–389–1335) is the big pull in the Popham area. You get there by taking Route 209 south out of Bath. To stay on Route 209, you have to make a left turn several miles out of Bath. If you miss the turn, you will be on what becomes Route 216 and wind up in **Small Point,** which isn't a bad place to be lost. Its **Head Beach** is a small swimming beach that you might want to check out, but Popham Beach is bigger and better for most travelers.

As you wind your way into Popham Beach, you should enjoy the country atmosphere. The entrance to the beach will be on your right, and it's well marked. This recreational area includes 3 miles of sandy beach to play on. Sandbars, tidal pools, and smooth rocks attract children just like bread crumbs pull in seagulls. But watch your young ones carefully, the undertow can be strong. An entrance fee of $1.50 is charged for adults. Children between the ages of five and eleven pay $.50; younger children get in free. The season for this beach is mid-April to mid-October, but don't expect to swim except during the warmer summer months. The water can be quite cold. This beach is not crowded, but it does attract most of the tourists in the area. If you want a secret place to enjoy as a native, continue driving past the entrance to the park and go until you can't go anymore. It's only a mile or so.

When you reach the end of Route 209, you will see **Fort Popham** in front of you, lobster boats to your left, and a sign pointing to **Percy's Store** on your right. Park at Percy's. A fee is charged for all-day parking, but it's cheap and this is the best place to leave your vehicle while you explore the fort and the hidden beach. Percy's store has a small restaurant on the water side, and take-out food is available for picnickers.

This beach is not known by many tourists. Locals spend their time fishing the surf for bluefish, and children love to chase after the thousands of bait fish that the blues chase into shore. You and your kids can kick back and relax here without all the roar of a typical tourist beach. If you want ice cream, Percy's store is the place to get it. They give huge servings for affordable fees. Don't forget Percy's restaurant, right on the beach; it produces plenty of good food for a fair price.

Once you've felt the sand between your toes, take the short stroll up the rocks to Fort Popham. The structure is semicircular in design and was never finished completely. The granite fort was built in 1861. It is open from Memorial Day to Labor Day. Kids like to climb on the ramparts and explore the dark (and often mosquito-filled) rooms that make up this waterfront fort. Spiral staircases made of granite allow access to some good lookout points. Except for some campgrounds, the fort and the beach are about all there is to this little hidden haven, but the trip is worthwhile.

If you retrace your steps back to Bath and get on Route 1, heading for the big green bridge, you can visit **Reid State Park** (207–371–2303). Turn right as soon as you've crossed the bridge. You'll see a stop sign in front of you. Turn left and head out Route 127. It's about 14 miles to the beach, but the drive is pleasant and relaxing with good views. When you see a rock on your right side that has an American flag on it, turn right. You're getting close to the park.

Reid State Park offers so much for families. Two sandy beaches provide a choice of swimming areas. Surf can be rough, but it is rarely dangerous. Rock outcroppings allow for plenty of climbing and long views through coin-operated binoculars. A special lagoon is situated below the sand dunes to give younger children a wave-free place to splash and play in warmer water. Don't turn the kids loose—the lagoon is not overly shallow, but it can be waded by adults in most areas without ever going in over your head. The temperature of sea water in Maine stays cold until late into the summer, but the protected lagoon warms quickly. Picnic tables are placed throughout the park, and endless tidal pools and other areas of exploration will keep the kids happy. A snack bar cranks out good food for a fair price, but watch out for the gulls. They love to steal french fries or any other food left lying around. Changing rooms and bathrooms are on the premises.

Parking is rarely a problem, though you may have to walk a ways in prime season. This park offers what feels like a commercial beach area, but it also gives visitors a taste of the wild Maine waterfront. Depending upon where you spend your time, you can enjoy a variety of settings. Entrance fees are $2.00 for adults and $.50 for kids over the age of five. The gates to this beach are open from mid-April to mid-October, basically from early morning until dusk.

Camp Seguin (207–371–2777), in the shadow of Reid State Park, is a good family setting to camp with a tent or small RV. Tidal pools at the camp prove intriguing to children. A long day at the beach can stir an appetite. If this happens with your group, leave the beach and go back to the intersection with the rock with the flag on it. Turn right on Route 127 and take a short ride out to **Five Islands.** When you reach the parking lot at the road, you will be at a working shoreline where there is some fantastic seafood to be enjoyed. Folks that prefer burgers will not be disappointed, and there's even ice cream available. Dine at the wharf and enjoy the salt air and views before cutting out of town for Wiscasset.

WISCASSET

On your way up Route 1 to Wiscasset, you will pass the **Taste of Maine Restaurant** (207–443–4554) on your right. It may have a large, inflatable crab on the roof. This is a favorite seafood spot for tourists and locals alike. Prices aren't cheap, but the food, especially the double-lobster deal, is delicious. A little farther up the road you can see the nest of an osprey to your right in the marshlands. As you continue towards Wiscasset, roadside vendors may be selling anything from seafood to blueberries. Route 1 is a favored route of tourists, and you can be sure to encounter a number of circumstances that may warrant a stop. This coastal route will bring you into contact with a number of gift and specialty shops as you head toward Wiscasset.

When you enter the town of **Wiscasset,** you will be greeted by a number of **antiques shops.** In the summer, traffic along the main street is stopped by a crossing officer to allow pedestrians, of which there are many, to browse through a variety of shops and stores. The **Sheepscot River** creates a beautiful backdrop for this delightful town. A favorite spot for photographers has been the water's edge, where the barely visible remnants of two wrecked nineteenth-century schooners, the *Hesper* and the *Luther Little*, sit close to shore.

Historic homes are available for your inspection. The **Musical Wonder House** (207–882–7163) at 18 High Street is one of these homes. It holds more interest for children than most house tours. An unusual collection of music boxes, reed organs, pump organs, and other music makers are housed here. When you take one of the daily guided tours, from mid-May to mid-October, the many musical wonders are played and demonstrated. The price of admission is $8.00 per person for a ground-floor tour. If you want to see the entire house, the price is $25 and you will need up to three hours to complete the tour. The house was home to a sea captain in 1852. Other historic homes in the area include the **Nickels-Sortwell House** at the corner of Maine and Federal Streets and **Castle Tucker** at the intersection of Lee and High Streets (207–882–7364).

The **Lincoln County Museum** (207–882–6817) on Federal Street is open in July and August. Tours are given from 11:00 A.M. to 4:00 P.M., at a cost of $2.00 per adult and $1.00 for children age twelve and under. The main attraction here is the old jail. It was built of thick granite walls in 1811 and used until 1913. The jailer's house was used until 1953. Tools and alternating exhibits are displayed, but the kids will probably find the jail more interesting.

If you like trains, you have to take a ride on the **Maine Coast Railroad** (207–882–8000). Located at the Wiscasset Town Landing on Water Street, this bright red, restored 1920s train will take you and your family on a stunning tour of the coastal countryside. The train runs from Memorial Day through Columbus Day at a cost of $10 per adult and $5 for kids between five and twelve years of age. Your whole family can ride for $25, if that's less expensive than the per-person rates. Your children will love seeing and photographing the wild Maine country. Wildlife and wildflowers are likely to be spotted, and the ride is fun even if the animals don't cooperate.

Downeast Flying Service (207–882–6752) in Wiscasset provides another way to see the sights. They'll take you up high above the ground for a bird's-eye view of what's below. A minimum of three passengers is required for the thirty-minute flights, at a rate of $50 for three people. The service operates Monday through Friday 8:00 A.M. to 5:00 P.M.

If the day's journey has stirred your appetite, one of the best places to eat in Wiscasset is **Le Garage** (207–882–5409). Located on Water Street close to the shipwrecks and train station, this restaurant offers views that are nearly as good as the food that is served. Lunch menus for soup and sandwiches are about $5.50. Light dinners start at less than $7.00, and more substantial dinners are less than $15.00. Seafood, pasta, and vegetarian selections are just part of the menu. The food and service is good, and children are welcome.

Hot dogs can be found on many streets in Maine villages, but **Red's Eats** is one such vendor that has served Wiscasset for more than six decades. Located on Water Street, just before the bridge, this hot-dog stand with tables and chairs will serve up a crab roll or hot dog in fast fashion. The stand is open from April through September. **Sarah's Pizza and Cafe** (207–882–7504) on the corner of Maine and Water Streets is open daily and serves what is probably the best pizza around. Mexican meals and lobster are also available. A quick trip across the bridge will put you at the **Muddy Rudder** (207–882–7748). It's open daily from 11:00 A.M. to 11:00 P.M. and serves steak and seafood. The setting is more formal than Red's Eats, but casual clothing is fine.

Lodging is sparse in Wiscasset, but you can find accommodations at the **Marston House** (207–882–6010) on Maine Street. It's a bed and breakfast with rates from $75. The **Edgecomb Inn** (207–882–6343) is just across the bridge from Wiscasset and offers competitive rates. **Cod Cove Inn** (207–882–9586), a little farther up Route 1 at the intersection of Route 27, has plenty of modern rooms. Rates range from $88 to $113 for a double.

EDGECOMB

Edgecomb is spread out along Route 27, which is a right turn off Route 1 just a short ways after crossing the bridge in Wiscasset. Route 27 will take you through Edgecomb and into **Boothbay Harbor,** a side trip you should take. As you drive towards Boothbay Harbor, you will pass dozens of shops along the way. Edgecomb is not a town where you are likely to spend a lot of time, but it's a nice place to pass through. Horse lovers might want to stop off at **Ledgewood Riding Stables** (207–882–6346) at the intersection of Route 27 and Old County Road; they offer trail riding at hourly rates.

THE BOOTHBAY REGION

The **Boothbay Region** is a major tourist attraction. You should allow several hours for this visit. As you are approaching the area, on Route 27, you may want to stop at the **Boothbay Railway Village** (207–633–4727). It's on the left side of the road and can't be missed. Narrow-gauge trains, both as exhibits and as rides, are the main attraction here. Twenty-seven exhibit buildings show all aspects of small-town life, antique cars, and trains. Your children might enjoy seeing the one-room schoolhouse and the blacksmith shop. They will certainly like the twenty-minute ride on *Boothbay Central,* a coal-fired narrow-gauge train that treks around 1½ miles of track. The village is open daily from 9:30 A.M. to 5:00 P.M. from mid–June through Labor Day. It continues to operate until Columbus Day, but it closes at 4:30 P.M. Admission is $6.00 per adult and $3.00 per child.

As you might imagine, water and boating is the theme of Boothbay Harbor. If you love water, boats, and a variety of shops, Boothbay is a good place to go. **Islander Cruises** (207–633–2500) at Pier Six, Fisherman's Wharf, runs cruises from May 20 to October 20. Seal watching is one of the main attractions with this line. **Cap'n Fish Boat Cruises** (207–633–3244) at Pier One operates from mid-May to mid-October, seven days a week. You can schedule a cruise for one, two, or three hours and hope to see seals, puffins, whales, and other aquatic attractions. You will recognize Cap'n Fish Boat Cruises by looking for the red ticket booth. Families who would rather catch fish than photograph them can go sportfishing for mackerel, tuna, shark, bluefish, or striped bass. Call **Breakaway Sportfishing Charters** (Pier 6, Fisherman's Wharf; 207–633–6990) to arrange a fishing trip.

Lodging opportunities in the Boothbay region are abundant. The local chamber of commerce lists about fifty facilities. Of all the choices, **Emma's Guest House and Cottages** (207–633–5287) offers about the best rates. A room for three to four people is priced at $35 to $50. Located at 110 Atlantic Avenue, the establishment offers water views and proximity to all the action in town. The **Lion's Den** (207–633–7367) at 106 Townsend Avenue also offers very reasonable rates.

If hunger pangs strike, head for **Ebb Tide** (627 Commercial Street; 207–633–5692). Follow your nose until you see the red-striped awning.

This establishment may bring back memories. It is decked out with knotty-pine walls and booths that many parents may remember from their younger days. Breakfast is served here all day, along with other meals, such as lobster, club sandwiches, and seafood platters. The homemade desserts are all the reason you need to come here. A quick fix for a growling stomach is **Brud's Hotdogs,** a Boothbay Harbor fixture for more than fifty years. Brud's cart is motorized, but you will usually find him in the center of town or on the east side of the harbor. Does homemade ice cream sound good? The **Downeast Ice Cream Factory** (207–633–2816) on the byway offers a make-your-own sundae buffet. Fixings for toppings are too numerous to mention, and real hot fudge can be used to top your homemade meal of ice cream. When you've enjoyed all the action in the Boothbay region, retrace your tracks on Route 27 to get back to Route 1.

NEWCASTLE AND DAMARISCOTTA

Maine has a long and beautiful coastline. You could spend weeks exploring it and never come close to seeing all there is to see. Families often have their favorite places, and Camden often appears on lists of preferred destinations. Rockland and Belfast also rate highly on some lists, and, though Damariscotta is not as well known as the other towns, it too has a lot to offer to parents and children.

Separated only by the Damariscotta River, neither Newcastle nor Damariscotta are big tourist attractions in a flashy way and yet people come to and through these towns in incredible numbers. Primarily attractive as the logical jumping-off points to many other desirable locations, such as Down East and the Pemaquid region, Newcastle and Damariscotta also offer attractions of their own.

Newcastle, for instance, is home to **St. Patrick's Church,** New England's oldest surviving Catholic church. Built in 1808 and listed on the National Register of Historic Places, the building has been restored in many ways and maintains its original Revere bell. If you and your children would like to visit this piece of history, you will find the church on Academy Road (Route 215), just north of Damariscotta Mills. Call (207) 865–1212 for information.

During the nineteenth century, Damariscotta was a major source of clay for brick-making. Kilns were set up along the Damariscotta River, and the product was shipped out by boat. The town of Damariscotta is proud to have one of the oldest remaining historic homes in Maine. The **Chapman-Hall House,** built in 1754, is on the corner of Main and Church Streets. Admission to the house is $1 per person. Tours are offered from mid-June to early September.

If you want to see this region from the air, call **Captain Harry Harden** (207–529–5524) for a ride in his seaplane. Otherwise, use your car to tour this area or enjoy a walking tour of the streets of the twin villages.

You might want to grab a bite to eat before you venture out of town on side trips. Many families like Damariscotta's **Backstreet Landing** (207–563–5666) behind the Elm Street Plaza. Seafood here is mouth-watering. Homemade soup is always a big hit, and chowders are a frequent favorite. Prices are reasonable, and the service is good. They are open 11:30 A.M. to 9:00 P.M. Saturday through Sunday. Your children will probably like eating at the **Salt Bay Cafe** (207–563–1666) on Main Street in Damariscotta. Looking more like a greenhouse than a restaurant, this establishment serves local seafood, steak, burgers, and many fried dishes, all at family prices.

If you're in the mood for something quick to eat, try **Zecchino's Submarines** (207–563–1999). This little sub shop is near the town landing in Damariscotta. In addition to subs, you can get chili, soup, and salads. When it's time for dessert, you have to go to **Round Top Ice Cream** (207–563–5307) on Business Route 1 in Damariscotta. Open 11:30 A.M. to 10:00 P.M. seven days a week from April to Columbus Day, you can't find a better place to please your palate with ice cream.

Head to Newcastle if you'd like to rent a room to call home as you visit attractions on the fringes of the twin towns. Several inns and B&Bs in the Newcastle area offer nice accommodations at moderate to expensive rates. The **Newcastle Inn** (207–563–5685) on River Road is known for both its outstanding food and romantic atmosphere. There is a no-smoking policy in effect. Rates range from $75 in the off season to $175 in season. **The Flying Cloud** (207–563–2484), also on River Road, is an 1840s sea captain's home. You can rent one of its five guest rooms and enjoy homemade goodies for breakfast. Rates range from $65 to $85 in the off season and $65 to $90 in season.

The **Glidden House** (207–563–1859) on Glidden Street is an old Victorian home on a quiet street within walking distance of shops in both Newcastle and Damariscotta. Most rooms have private baths, and there is one three-room apartment. A double room with private bath will set you back about $60. The apartment rents for $75.

Another family-friendly lodging option in the Damariscotta area is the Oyster Shell Motel (Business Route 1, Darmariscotta; 800–874–3747). This low-key "resort" motel has a swimming pool and features one- and two-bedroom suites that overlook the salt bay. Rates range from $59 to $85 in the off season and $85 to $109 in season.

Deciding where to go when you depart Damariscotta can pose a dilemma: You can go east to Pemaquid Point (a good choice), you can head west to Damariscotta Lake, or, you can continue your way up the coast on Route 1. Since Pemaquid Point is so popular, let's head in that direction first.

PEMAQUID POINT

To get to Pemaquid Point, you will drive out of Damariscotta on Route 130. This will take you through the town of Bristol, in the vicinity of Round Pond (where Captain Kidd's treasure may be buried), through the town of New Harbor, and eventually to the end of land at the point. You can also branch out on Route 129 and travel along the Damariscotta River through Walpole, West Bristol, South Bristol, and Christmas Cove. On the way back from the point, you can pick up Route 32 in New Harbor and enjoy a scenic drive along the coast of Muscongus Sound. This will take you right past Round Pond, through several other picturesque towns, and connect you back with U.S. Route 1.

No matter how you decide to tour the area, make sure you plan a stop at the **Thompson Ice House** (207–644–8551) on Route 129 in Bristol. Here modern families can see slide shows and videos that explain how this 150-year-old family business continues to harvest ice the old-fashioned way. You can also see the tools of the ice trade. It's open in July and August, on Wednesday, Friday, and Saturday from 1:00 to 4:00 P.M. An entry fee is charged. Adults pay $1.00; children pay $.50.

When you leave Bristol, continue on Route 130 to **New Harbor,** perhaps one of the most photogenic working harbor towns in Maine. New Harbor is home to Pemaquid Beach and is also next to the Rachel Carson Salt Pond Reserve. **Pemaquid Beach** (207–677–2754) is open from Memorial Day to Labor Day from 9:00 A.M. to 5:00 P.M. Children under twelve are admitted at no charge, but adults pay a use fee of $1.00 each. You will find rest rooms, picnic areas, a bathhouse, and a concession stand at the beach. This is a good swimming beach, but sea breezes are often strong here, so consider bringing jackets with you.

The Rachel Carson Salt Pond Reserve covers seventy-eight acres. It consists of a small cove, a tidal salt pond, many trees, and granite outcroppings. Parking is provided at a scenic lookout. The reserve is just outside of New Harbor, on Route 32.

If you have time for a delightful cruise while you're in town, call the **Hardy Boat** (207–677–2026). You can depart New Harbor in search of puffins on **Monhegan Island** or take a sunset cruise to Pemaquid Point. Seals and other marine life are often sighted on the trips. You may also want to ask about the clambakes that are held on Monhegan Island.

You'll be hungry after a tour by car or boat. Keep in mind that seafood is king in this part of Maine. **Shaw's** (207–677–2200), a local lobster pound and favorite feeding spot, is a wonderful place to take the kids for fresh seafood on a dock. The food flows freely from late May to mid-October. Lobster and steamed clams are the cream of the crop, but you can get meatloaf, turkey, and assorted stews and sandwiches if you're not in the mood for seafood. Choose between the inside dining room and the picnic tables on the dock. Watch out for the seagulls if you eat outside. They will steal your food if you are not careful.

Another New Harbor eatery is **Captain's Catch Seafood** (207–677–2396). Located on the Pemaquid Beach Road, this place is known for its picnic-style dining on seafood and homemade desserts. Open 11:00 A.M. to 8:00 P.M. daily during the summer, you can eat indoors or out. There is a fish fry on Fridays.

Colonial Pemaquid State Historic Site (207–677–2423) off Route 130 in **Pemaquid** is an interesting place to spend some time with your kids. It's open from Memorial Day to Labor Day, from 9:30 A.M. to 5:00 P.M. Kids under five and adults over sixty-five get in for free. Ages five through eleven pay only $.50 and adults pay $2.00. A settlement was built here in the early 1600s, and you can still see an old burial ground dating back to 1695. Children can see the artifacts of many years ago in this in-the-field museum.

Your admission to the Historic Site also buys you admission to **Fort William Henry,** also off Route 130. Built in 1907, this replica fort (the original was built in 1698) is typical of a series of English fortifications used to defend against pirates and the French. A stockade was erected in 1630, but Dixie Bull, the pirate, destroyed it promptly. In 1689, Baron Castine captured the fortification that was manned by fifty men. It's open from Memorial Day to Labor Day.

The Pemaquid Point Lighthouse (207–677–2494) at the end of Route 130 is open to the public for a fee. Kids under twelve get in at no charge; adults pay $1.00, and seniors are charged $.50. This lighthouse was built in 1824. Keep your children away from the waves that can be rough along the rocks, but let them dabble in the numerous tidal pools. This fascinating activity can occupy a child for hours as they discover the small marine creatures that inhabit the pools.

While you are at the point, you can visit the **Fishermen's Museum.** You will find model ships, photographs, and artifacts of the Maine fishing industry here. It is open from Memorial Day to Columbus Day. Hours are 10:00 A.M. to 5:00 P.M., Monday through Saturday, and 11:00 A.M. to 5:00 P.M. on Sundays. While you're here, you can picnic on the museum grounds or eat at the nearby **Sea Gull Shop and Restaurant** (207–677–2374). If you enjoy local art, check out the **Pemaquid Art Gallery,** also on the point.

The fishing village of **Round Pond** has the reputation of once being home to pirates. Rumor has it that the infamous Captain Kidd may have buried treasure in the **Devil's Oven,** near New Harbor. This inlet area was once a major shipbuilding location, and it remains an active fishing spot for lobstermen and commercial fishermen.

If you get hungry while in search of Captain Kidd's footprints, stop in at the **Anchor Inn** (207–529–5584) in Round Pond. It's open from Memorial Day through Columbus Day for lunch and dinner. As you sit in the tiered dining room, you will have a commanding view of the harbor and village. The view alone is worth the trip, but you won't be disappointed by the

Pemaquid Point Lighthouse is a great place to get out and stretch those legs.
(Courtesy Maine Office of Tourism)

food or service. As you might imagine, seafood is the leader of the menu.

Inns, B&Bs, and cottages are for rent to overnight guests throughout the villages and towns in this region. The **Gosnold Arms** (207–677–3727), for instance, is on Route 32 in New Harbor. Open from mid-May through mid-October, it is situated across the road from the water. This inn has been putting up guests since 1925, and all of its eleven guest rooms have private baths. In addition to the rooms, more than a dozen cottages on the property are available to guests. This is not a pretentious place, but it's large, clean, comfortable, and has a homey feeling. Rooms rent for $75 to $94 for a double. Cottages go for $98 to $124.

Bradly Inn (207–677–2105) at 361 Pemaquid Point in New Harbor is open from April through January 2. A dozen guest rooms, each with a private bath, are available in this turn-of-the-century inn. You and your kids can rent bicycles to pedal down to the lighthouse. Upper-level rooms have a view of John's Bay. Rates range from $85 to $120 off season and $100 to $195 in season.

The hamlet of **Christmas Cove** in the town of South Bristol is the setting for **Coveside Inn** (207–644–8282). Here you have a choice of traditional inn rooms or more modern, motel-like accommodations. The five traditional rooms all have private baths, and ten motel units line the shore on the opposite side of the road from the main inn. The modern rooms have vaulted ceilings, skylights, and decks. Rooms in the inn are $75. You will have to pay $90 dollars for a double in the modern rooms.

The **Hotel Pemaquid** (207–677–2312) sits less than 200 feet from Pemaquid Point, but it has no water views. The interior views are pretty, though; a Victorian theme is played out well in this inn. Many rooms have private baths, but some don't. You will be in easy walking distance of the **Sea Gull Restaurant,** which overlooks the ocean. The inn has a no-smoking policy, and rates start at less than $50 a night in the off-season. In-season rates can be much higher.

If you enjoy the flair of a bed and breakfast, try the **Apple Tree B&B** (207–677–3491) in New Harbor, within walking distance of Pemaquid Beach and Fort William Henry. Rates are about $70 for a double during prime season. Another nice, affordable B&B is **The Briar Rose** (207–529–5478) in Round Pond. It offers good views of the harbor just down the road, and antique furnishings make each room interesting. The off-season rate is around $30; the in-season rate is $70.

If you are planning an extended stay or require substantial room, you can look into the availability of some cottages. **Thompson House and Cottages** (207–677–2317) is one option in New Harbor. **Ye Olde Forte Cabins** (207–677–2261) at Pemaquid Beach is another possibility. If you are willing to stay at least a week, **The Jamestown** (207–677–3677) in Pemaquid Beach is an affordable and nice place to stay, but a one-week minimum is required for these cottages.

When you are ready to head back to the main coastal route, which is U.S. Route 1, you should take Route 32. This very scenic drive is always pleasant. When you reach the intersections of Route 32 and Route 1, you can either turn right on Route 1 and continue up the coast through **Waldoboro** or stay on Route 32 until you get to **Jefferson.** Neither town is far out of your way, and Damariscotta Lake in Jefferson offers some good warm-water fishing opportunities. You can rent a boat and motor from **Damariscotta Lake Farm** (207–549–7953) if you want to get out on the lake. **Damariscotta Lake State Park** on Route 32 in Jefferson has a sand beach on the lake. You can swim, picnic, fish, or hike at the beach and park. True landlubbers may want to forgo the lake and go trail riding on horseback at **Tide's End Riding Stables** (207–832–4431) in Waldoboro.

ROCKLAND

Rockland is the next major stop along the mid-coast route. A good-sized town with a very busy waterfront, it is said to be one of the busiest lobster distribution points in the world. Many good activities will keep the kids happy in Rockland and its surrounding towns.

Begin your adventure at the **Shore Village Museum** (207–594–0311) at 104 Limerock Street. This museum has something for everyone. Children with an interest in the United States Coast Guard can see a variety of old artifacts. All sorts of lighthouse stuff can be seen—foghorns, flashing lights, bells, boats, and buoys are all part of the collection. Civil War memorabilia may not be expected in such a place, but it's here. Anyone with an interest in dolls will love the large collection on display. The dolls are dressed in period costumes right up to the Gay Nineties. The museum is open from June to mid-October. You can get in seven days a week from 10:00 A.M. to 4:00 P.M. and by appointment. Admission is free but donations are accepted.

If the kids need to burn off some energy in a hurry, take them to the **Rockland Skate Center** (207–594–1023) at 299 Park Street. They can go roller skating here. Or, take them to **Rockland Breakwater Light,** a lighthouse on Samoset Road, to let them run around a bit. Parking here is free, and there is plenty of space for walking and stretching cramped muscles.

Maine has more lighthouses than any other coastal state. **Penobscot Bay** is said to have the largest number of lighthouses in the state. One light that is worth a short side trip is the **Owls Head Light.** This is not in Rockland, but in nearby Owl's Head. Take Route 73 to North Shore Drive Road. Go about 2 miles. When you get to the intersection by a small post office, turn left down Main Street. Drive about one-quarter of a mile and turn left, onto Lighthouse Drive. This road turns to dirt, but it's very passable. Built in 1825, Owls Head Light commands attention from its rocky perch. There are sheer cliffs here, so keep close reins on your kids. There are, however, safe trails down one side to the rocks below.

While you are in Owls Head, stop by the **Owls Head Transportation Museum** (207–594–4418). It's off Route 73, adjacent to the Knox County Airport. Founded in 1974, this museum is open 10:00 A.M. to 4:00 P.M. seven days a week and charges an admission of $6.00 for adults, $5.00 for families, $4.00 for children five to twelve, children under five get in free. The museum specializes in old planes and automobiles. What makes it different from most museums is that all of the displays still function. Exhibitions are put on during some weekends where you might see a 1918 plane in the air or a 1901 car on the road. Rides are occasionally offered in some cases. If it has wheels, you will probably find it here. Now, back to Rockland.

What would a coastal town be without boat trips? If you and your family enjoy riding the waves, Rockland is an excellent place to launch from. There are lighthouse cruises, water taxis, fishing boats, and other vessels to ride on. The *Henrietta* (207–594–5411) is a deep-sea fishing boat that leaves about 7:30 A.M. and returns around 4:30 P.M. The *Pauline* (800–999–7352) takes off from Windjammer Wharf. It is an 83-foot motor vessel that offers week-long tours of the coastline. Up to twelve guests can go aboard at one time. Accommodations are luxurious, but the seven-day cruises come with big price tags. Expect to spend about $775–$950 per person, all meals included.

If you don't want to spend a week or a grand to see the shore, you can opt for some other boating offers. The *Annie McGee* (207–594–9049) will take up to six passengers out for day trips. This is a sailboat. *Wendameen* (207–236–3472) is a 67-foot schooner that will take you out for an overnight trip. **Atlantic Expeditions** (207–372–8621) will take you out on the 50-foot *Finback* to sail to **Matinicus Rock** and **Seal Island National Wildlife Refuge.** This is a day trip with seals and puffins as the main attractions. *M/V Monhegan* (207–596–5660) runs lunch and dinner cruises as well as harbor tours. Curious about lobster fishing? Take a ride on *The Three Cheers* (207–594–0900) to do some real lobstering and to see the lighthouses.

Windjammer cruises are increasing in popularity. Rockland is harbor to many for-hire windjammers. Trips usually run from three to six days and cost from $300 to $700 per person. Some boats have higher rates. Off-season rates are usually lower than prime season, which is July and August. This is an expensive vacation amusement, but when you consider the cost of lodging and food elsewhere, it may not be such a bad deal. Most of the boats are not fancy, but they provide the essentials. If you want a once-in-a-lifetime memory for your kids, this might be just the ticket.

The **American Eagle** (800–648–4544) is at the North End Shipyard. She is a 92-foot vessel that can accommodate twenty-eight guests in fourteen double cabins. This boat has an engine and comfortable quarters down below. Rates run $705 for a six-day cruise and $395 for a three-day cruise. The **Isaac H. Evans** (800–648–4544) is also out of North End Shipyard. This craft is 65 feet with eleven double cabins and a total guest capacity of twenty-two. Rates run $705 for a six-day cruise and $370 for a

Victory Chimes *will take you out for a day on the water.* (Courtesy Maine Office of Tourism)

three-day cruise. The *Heritage* (207–594–8007) out of North End Ship-yard is a newer schooner. Built in 1980, it is a 95-footer that can take on thirty-three passengers. Rates are between $635 and $705 for a six-day cruise.

J & E Riggin (800–869–0604) is an 89-foot vessel. The *Stephen Taber* (800–999–7352) out of Windjammer Wharf is 68 feet long. This boat was first launched in 1871 and is the oldest documented United States sailing vessel in continuous use. The *Victory Chimes* (800–745–5651) is the only original three-masted schooner in the wind-jammer trade. At 170 feet, it is also the largest. There are other ships in town, of course, but they are too numerous to mention. If you would like more information, you can contact the **Maine Windjammer Association** at (800) 807–WIND or at P.O. Box 1144, Blue Hill, Maine, 04614.

When you return to dry land and need lodging before you leave town, Rockland has a few B&Bs you might have an interest in. The **Captain Lindsey House** (5 Lindsey Street; 207–596–7950) offers rooms in the $100 range. **Old Granite Inn** (546 Main Street; 207–594–9036) is a mansion that was built in the 1840s. This granite building is attached to a 1790s wooden Cape Cod. Twelve comfortable guest rooms have rich woodwork that is often a topic of conversation. Only three of the rooms have private baths. Rates run from less than $50 to about $100.

The LimeRock Inn (96 Limerock Street; 207–594–2257) is another option, but it tends to be expensive. **The Mermaid** (256 Main Street; 207–594–0616) is an old Colonial home. Weekly rates are around $250. Two motels worth looking into are the **Trade Winds** (2 Parkview Drive; 207–596–6661) and **The Navigator** (520 Main Street; 207–594–2131).

Hot-dog lovers will want to track down **Wasses Wagon.** It is usually at 2 North Main Street or at the corner of Park and Union Streets. **The Brown Bag** (207–596–6372) is both casual and affordable. The food is good, and there's an extensive menu. For variety, however, the **Landings Restaurant and Pub** (207–596–6563) is hard to beat. You can eat indoors or out when you arrive at 1 Commercial Street. The restaurant is right on the harbor, and you can get hot dogs, steak, lobster, or most any-thing else you might want.

If none of these ideas fan your appetites, you can try **Jessica's: A**

European Bistro (2 South Main Street; 207–596–0770). Reservations are recommended. Continental cuisine includes meat, seafood, and pasta. Prices are moderate. Another good choice is **Cafe Miranda** (15 Oak Street; 207–594–2034). Make reservations here, because area residents fill this fine food establishment quickly. Prices are on the low end of moderate, and you can enjoy seafood, pasta, and a lot of other good stuff.

If you feel like taking in a movie while you are in Rockland, see what's showing at **The Strand Cinema** (207–594–7266) on Main Street. Dozens of antique shops for you to browse through are in the Rockland area, as are numerous other stores of interest. Plan on spending a little time poking around the local shops for fun and souvenirs. Once you are ready to leave, head up Route 1 toward Rockport and Camden. You're in for a treat.

CAMDEN

Before you approach Camden on Route 1, you will pass through the town of **Rockport.** While Camden is probably the most popular tourist attraction in this area, places like Rockport and Lincolnville (farther down Route 1) all have something to offer. If you plan to spend some time in this area, Camden is a good place to call home for awhile. Make reservations early, however—this town fills up fast.

The **Old Conway House Complex** (207–236–2257) lies just off Route 1 south of Camden. Open during July and August, this eighteenth-century farmhouse is furnished to represent many periods. Kids can see carriages, sleighs, and early farm tools. A blacksmith shop on the property is often the most intriguing exhibit to children. Adults are charged $2.00, and children over six pay $.50

The **Knox Mill Museum** on Mechanic Street in Camden, documents 125 years of operation of the Knox Woolen Mill. You can see a film, pictures, and some machinery. Hours are 9:00 A.M. to 5:00 P.M., weekdays only.

Fred's Bikes (207–236–6664) at 53 Chestnut Street rents all sorts of bikes. You can get mountain bikes, touring bikes, kiddie carts, and so forth. There is even a delivery service that will bring the bikes to you. Fred's is open 10:00 A.M. to 5:00 P.M. in the winter and 9:00 A.M. to 6:00 P.M. in the summer.

Golfers can go to **Goose River Golf Club** (207–236–8488) on Simonton Road for a quick nine holes. Cart rentals are available. An eighteen-hole course that has gained much publicity is the **Samoset Golf Course** (207–594–2511) in Rockport. Many of the fairways run along the water, and the views are outstanding. Carts are available. This same facility offers tennis courts for both indoor and outdoor play.

If you feel the need for some time in the gym, you can go to the **YMCA** (207–236–3375) at 50 Chestnut Street. A small day-use fee is charged for use of the Olympic-size pool, weight room, and basketball court.

If you prefer to swim outside the confines of a pool, you're in luck. **Laite Memorial Park and Beach** at upper Bayview Street offers saltwater swimming. Freshwater swimming can be found off Route 52, northwest of Camden, in **Megunticook Lake.** You can also swim at **Shirttail Beach** on Route 105 outside of Camden and the **Willis Hodson Park** on the Megunticook River at the Molyneaux Road.

Since Camden is a harbor town, boating is big business here. Many businesses offer boat excursions and windjammer cruises. You don't have to look far to find a boat for hire. Even kayaks and canoes are available.

Cruises of all types are available on many boats. **Figaro Cruises** (800–473–6169) does three- and six-day cruises. The *Appledore* (207–236–8353) is an 86-foot schooner that is said to have sailed around the world. These days, it takes passengers out for day trips. The *Surprise* (207–236–4687) is a 57-foot schooner that gives terrific two-hour rides. The *Olad* (207–236–2323) also gives two-hour trips. The *Betselma* (207–236–2101) offers one-hour sight-seeing tours. Windjammer cruises typically run for several days. If you are interested in an extended cruise, contact the **Maine Windjammer Association** (800–807–WIND), for a complete listing of opportunities.

Winter in Camden offers skiing at **Camden Snow Bowl** (207–236–3438) on Hosmer's Pond Road. Trails suitable for beginners and experts are available. Night skiing is offered. The facilities include a lodge, cafeteria, and a rental and repair shop.

Camden Hills State Park (207–236–3109) on Route 1 also provides skiing opportunities in winter. This is cross-country skiing on marked and maintained trails. In warmer weather, you can enjoy other activities at the park. This 6,500-acre area includes **Mount Megunticook,** one of the highest points on the Atlantic seaboard. More than one hundred campsites provide accommodation for tenters in the park, and hiking is the number-one attraction. Excellent trails suitable for the whole family take you to the park's most scenic spots. Day-use admission for adults is $2.00; children aged six to twelve are charged $.50 cents; younger kids get in free.

Are you looking for a little culture? The **Camden Civic Theatre** (207–236–2281) can provide it. Located on Main Street, this theater shows a wide variety of theatrical performances. Tickets are priced reasonably, and you can count on a good show. If you want to backtrack to Rockport, you can go to the **Rockport Opera House** (207–236–2823) and take in the **Bay Chamber Concerts.** July and August offer concerts on Thursday and Friday evenings.

Art galleries are numerous in this area. The three to visit in Camden are **Harbor Square Gallery** at 58 Bayview Street, **Pine Tree Shop and Bay View Gallery** on Bayview Street, and **A Small Wonder Gallery** on Commercial Street. Rockport offers the **Maine Coast Artists Gallery,** on Russell Avenue.

Whether you've been hiking, sailing, or just cruising the galleries, you're bound to be hungry at some point. Camden has lots of places to satisfy the family appetite. **Cappy's Chowder House** (207–236–2254) at 1 Main Street likes kids. Your children will get their own menu, a souvenir carrying box, a place mat with puzzles, and crayons for coloring. Sometimes balloons round out the kiddie package. From eggs to burgers to granola and, of course, to chowder, you can put on a good eat at a fair price here.

Scott's Place (207–236–8751) at 85 Elm Street is easy to miss, but you really shouldn't pass it by. For quality food and very low prices, this is the place to be. Kids can have hot dogs for less than $1.00. Succulent lobster rolls cost about $6.00. Marinated chicken, burgers, and other yummy stuff dot the menu. It's a take-out stand in the parking lot of a shopping center, but don't let the appearance fool you. This small place is big on good food and tiny prices.

Ayer's Fish Market (207–236–3509) on Main Street has what may be the best, and least expensive, fish chowder around. For about $1.50, you can lunch on a generous bowl of tasty chowder. Lobster and other good foods are also available.

Would you like to have a lobster picnic delivered to you at the harbor park or town landing? Call **Captain Andy's** at (207–236–2312) and your dream will come true. You can choose from about thirty-five different sandwiches at the **Camden Deli** (207–236–8343) on Main Street. Another good deli is **Fitzpatrick's Deli Cafe** (207–236–2041) at Sharp's Wharf on Bayview Street. Many other good eateries are located in the hub of Camden, and they're not hard to find.

According to what I've heard, there are more than twenty bed and breakfasts in Camden. This seems like a lot, but most don't have a great number of rooms, so the town fills up fast. Many of the B&Bs require a minimum stay of two nights. Rooms rates range from as little as $85 for a double to $200 or more.

One of the best bargains in town is **The Owl and Turtle Harbor View Guest Rooms** (207–236–9014) at 8 Bayview Street. As the name implies, the harbor views are excellent. With high-end prices of $85, this is one of the least expensive places to stay. Unfortunately, the three guest rooms book quickly. Call well in advance, and you may get the chance to stay here.

Most of the inns and B&Bs are competitive in both quality and price. Some of the ones you may wish to inquire further are the **Belmont** (207–236–8053), **Whitehall Inn** (207–236–3391), **Camden Harbour Inn** (207–236–4200), the **Blue Harbor House** (207–236–3196), **Hartstone Inn** (207–236–4259), **The Maine Stay** (207–236–9636), **Hawthorn Inn** (207–236–8842), **Windward House** (207–236–9656), and **The Blackberry Inn** (207–236–6060).

BELFAST

As you continue along Route 1 up the coast, you will pass through **Lincolnville** and **Northport** on your way to **Belfast.** Other little towns with items of interest along the way include **Prospect, Orland, Liberty,** and **Frankfort.** Belfast doesn't get all the hype that Boothbay Harbor, Camden, and Bar Harbor get. Don't let this fool you. Belfast may prove to be one of your favorite spots. Let me tell you why.

Perry's Tropical Nut House (207–338–1630) on Route 1 just east

ROGER'S FAVORITE FAMILY ADVENTURES IN MID-COAST MAINE

Pemaquid Beach, New Harbor; 207–677–2754
Colonial Pemaquid State Historic Site, Pemaquid;
  207–677–2423
The Pemaquid Point Lighthouse, Pemaquid; 207–677–2494
Shore Village Museum, Rockland; 207–594–0311
Perry's Tropical Nut House, Belfast; 207–338–1630
Belfast and Moosehead Lake R.R. Co., Belfast; 207–338–2330
Craig Brook National Fish Hatchery, Ellsworth; 207–469–2801
Camden Hills State Park, Camden; 207–236–3109
Maine Windjammer Association, Camden; 1–800–807–WIND
Owls Head Transportation Museum, Owls Head;
  207–594–4418

of Belfast is not what you might expect to find in Maine. In fact, you might not expect to find anything like this anywhere. Irving Perry started the place back in the 1920s. He wanted to sell pecans to passing tourists. In doing so, he collected every type of nut known to humankind. These nuts were put on display to pull in the pecan trade. Nuts were not the only items he collected and showed off. Even today, long after Perry's passing, his stuffed alligators, monkeys, ostriches, gorillas, and similar exotic animals are still open to public view. This is a good place to stop for pictures with the kids.

The **Belfast Museum** (207–338–2078) at 10 Market Street will not appeal to all children, but it does offer exhibits of area artifacts, paintings, and similar works. Going up in an airplane might be more fun, and certainly more memorable for a young child. **Ace Aviation, Inc.** (207–338–2970) offers scenic rides with a two-person minimum. Flights leave from Belfast Municipal Airport.

The **Belfast City Park** on Route 1 has a swimming pool, tennis courts, and a gravel beach. Picnic areas are also available to you and your family. Art galleries can be found on both Main and High Streets in Belfast. Bookstores are on Main Street, and other specialty shops round out the shopping entertainment.

Do you remember the **Weathervane** restaurant in Kittery? There's another one in Belfast. It's at the **City Landing,** and you call it at (207) 338–1774. From burgers to lobster, you won't be disappointed. **Young's Lobster Pound** (207–338–1160) may have 30,000 lobsters on hand to take care of the most hearty eaters. There is a great view of the **Passagassawakeag River** that you can take in while you wait for your meal. This spot is on Mitchell Avenue, just across the bridge from Belfast.

The rates for lodging in Belfast are considerably lower than they are in Camden. The low-end rates start around $40, with higher rates reaching the $85 range. The **Alden House Bed and Breakfast** (207–338–2151) at 63 Church Street is a good-looking place with eight guest rooms. Most rooms share a bath.

A more expensive, but still reasonable, place to stay the night is the **Jeweled Turret Inn** (207–338–2304) at 40 Pearl Street. Each of the seven guest rooms has a private bath. Hardwood floors and fancy beds add to the charm of this inn.

Before you leave Belfast, consider taking a train ride on the **Belfast and Moosehead Lake R.R. Co.** (207–338–2330). The train leaves for a two-and-a-half-hour excursion from the Belfast waterfront along the Passagassawakeag River. It runs from May through October. You will go to the little village of Brooks and back. Along the way, the infamous **"Waldo Station Gang"** will attempt a train robbery. Kids love this, although some youngsters may be frightened by the authenticity of this staged event. Other train activities include a rail-and-sail package, where you ride both the train and the *Voyageur,* an old Mississippi steamboat. The steamboat ride tours the southern part of the **Penobscot River.**

SEARSPORT

The next town you come to along the coastal route is **Searsport.** The **Penobscot Marine Museum** (207–548–2529) is located here on Route 1. Housed in the 1845 town hall, the museum attractions track the evolution of sailing vessels from the seventeenth century. Other exhibits show how local people made their livings around the bay. This includes working with granite, lime, ice, and fishing. A gift shop provides souvenirs. Open daily from Memorial Day through mid-October, the museum hours are Monday through Saturday from 9:30 A.M. to 5:00 P.M. and Sundays from 1:00 to 5:00 P.M. Adults must pay $5.00; kids aged seven to fifteen pay $1.50.

For outdoor fun, you might try the **Mosman Beach Park** at the town dock in Searsport. It offers a public boat ramp, and you can go fishing or swimming for free. A good picnic spot is the **Moose Point State Park** on Route 1 just south of Searsport. Cookout facilities, fields, and an evergreen grove await you.

The **Waldo County Co-Op** on Route 1 in Searsport Harbor offers crafts for sale. Dolls, needlepoint, quilts, pillows, jams, wooden items, and lots of ceramics provide great ideas for gifts and mementos of your trip. It's open daily from June to October. If the goods at the co-op don't meet your needs, **Silkweeds** (207–548–6501) on Route 1 also has a lot of country crafts. Antiques lovers can't pass up the **Searsport Antiques Mall.** This place is open daily all year and represents the wares of seventy-some dealers. About thirty other antiques shops are in the area, as are flea markets to browse through for treasures. Just ride up Route 1, and you will see them.

You may need to replace a few calories after swimming or treasure hunting. Searsport provides great establishments to nourish you. **Nickerson Tavern** (207–548–2220) on Route 1 is a tasty place to eat. The entrees are moderately priced, and the food, service, and atmosphere are perfect. Choose from veal and mushrooms, chicken, shrimp, or any of the other items on the extensive menu. Nickerson Tavern is seasonal; it's open Easter through New Years. **Light's Diner** (207–548–2405) is not fancy, but its orange booths give it color, and the food is memorable. A full salad bar is one of its trademarks; affordable prices make it great for families.

The **Seafarer's Tavern** (207–548–2465) on Route 1 serves lunch and dinner, except on Sunday. Sandwiches, ribs, chicken, and pizza are some of what you will find on the affordable menu. **Jordan's Restaurant** (207–548–2555), also on Route 1, serves all three meals in classic style. You can eat in or take it out, and from beef to seafood to a special menu for kids, you can find it here.

Need a place to rest your head for a night or two? Searsport can help you out in this way, too. Lodging rates in Searsport are similar to those affordable rates in Belfast. The **Homeport Inn** (800–742–5814) on Route 1 is open all year. This 1861 captain's mansion overlooks the bay. Ten gorgeous rooms are available for rent. Some rooms share a bath; others have a private one. At $30 for a single and $75 for a double, the charges here are quite reasonable. A two-bedroom cottage on the property rents for $500 a week.

Other good places to stay include the **Captain Green Pendleton B&B** (207–548–6523) on Route 1. Eight acres of grounds, a cross-country ski trail, and a private pond make this option attractive to families. The **Thurston House B&B Inn** (207–548–2213) at 8 Elm Street can accommodate a family of five in one of their guest rooms. This vintage 1830s house posts rates of $40 to $60, including breakfast. It's hard to beat. You might also try the **Captain Butman Homestead** (207–548–2506), the **Summerwood Inn** (207–548–2202), and the **Carriage House Inn** (207–548–2289). All of these places are suitable for families, and their rates are mostly moderate.

STOCKTON SPRINGS

It's not much to look at on a map, but **Stockton Springs** is a pretty place to spend some time. Like many of the coastal areas in Maine, it's not big and doesn't show a lot of fanfare. It has some features, however, that are worth your attention. For example, the **Sandy Point Beach** just off Route 1 north of Stockton Springs is a great place to jump in the water on a hot day. To get here, turn off Route 1 and head for the water when you see the Rocky Ridge Motel. There are no facilities, but this place will bring back your memories of the old swimming hole you knew (or dreamed about) as a child and it will create new memories for your children.

You might want to tour **Fort Pownall** and **Fort Point State Park.** Both are off Route 1 in Stockton Springs. They're less than 4 miles off the main road, and signs lead you to them. In 1759 the forts were built to defend Maine from the British. After being burned twice, only earthworks remain. A park on the tip of the peninsula juts into **Penobscot Bay.** A favorite fishing and picnic spot, it features a lighthouse and a pier. It's worth going a little out of your way to reach this spot.

If you need sustenance, the place to eat in Stockton Springs is the **Sail Inn** on Route 1. It will serve you anything from deep-fried chicken and seafood to pizza and sandwiches. It's open from 7:00 A.M. to 8:00 P.M. You will find it just south of Fort Knox and the Verona Island Bridge.

If you're sleepy, check into the **Hichborn Inn** (207–567–4183) on Church Street. Rates run from $60 to $85 a night. If you're looking for atmosphere you'll find it here. Dad will enjoy the "Gent's parlor," where evening fires burn and men come to talk. This Victorian Italianate mansion is open all year, except for Christmas. Water views are standard equipment, and the accommodations are quite comfortable.

Once you are content to hit the road, you can start your engine and head Down East. Grab your map and head for the region that boasts of Bar Harbor and Acadia National Park.

1

1A

1

Ellsworth

Lamoine
Beach

Milbridge

Steuben

Jonesboro

1

Machias

Lubec

Machiasport

Jonesport
Beals Island

3

Bar Harbor

Great Wass
Island

ACADIA
NATIONAL
PARK

Stonington

Down East Maine

Down East Maine

Many people will tell you that you haven't been to Maine until you've been Down East. Certainly many sights and activities throughout the state deserve your attention, but Down East is a big part of Maine's reputation. Bar Harbor is probably the most famous town in Down East, and Acadia is synonymous with Down East. They're just two of the places you will want to go. There's a lot more to do, so let's talk about it.

ELLSWORTH

When you are ready to leave Stockton Springs, your next major destination is Ellsworth, the gateway to Down East and Acadia. You will be taking Route 1, which is also Route 3, from Stockton Springs to Ellsworth. When you arrive, you'll find attractions that are worth the drive.

Along your way to Ellsworth, you will pass through the town of Orland. Your kids might enjoy a brief side trip here. Turn off Route 1 in Orland, just east of Bucksport, and to the **Craig Brook National Fish Hatchery** (207–469–2801) in East Orland. It's open early in the morning and doesn't close until late afternoon. This salmon hatchery, established in 1871, is something to see. Aquariums, nature trails, an old icehouse, and picnic tables make this is a good place to take a break from traveling for a short while.

Once you arrive in Ellsworth, you can go to the **Birdsacre Sanctuary** (207–667–8460) on Route 3. This 130-acre preserve is set aside for birds and other wildlife. You and your family can explore a number of trails within the complex. Wildflowers, nesting birds, ponds, and much more can be seen along the trails, which are mostly easy and suitable for almost anyone.

The family may also enjoy a visit to the **Colonel Black Mansion** (81 West Main Street; 207–667–8671), a Georgian-type period home richly furnished with authentic period furniture. It also features beautiful gardens and hiking trails. Open 10:00 A.M. to 5:00 P.M. June through October.

Lamoine Beach State Park in Ellsworth is not your typical tourist trap. In fact, it is one of the better-kept secrets of the region. Near the end of Route 184 at **Frenchman Bay,** it features a safe beach for swimming. Camping can be arranged for a small fee. Call (207) 667–4778 in the off season or (207) 941–4014 in season for information.

Some of you may prefer indoor exercise. The **YMCA** invites you to work out at their facility on State Street. A pool, a gymnasium, and a fitness center offer plenty of opportunities for the whole family. You can call (207) 667–3086 for more details. There is no time like the present to get and stay fit.

Ellsworth is a good place to stop for the night when you are making your way into Down East Maine. Lodging is reasonable, and good food is easy to find. The **Brookside Motel** (207–667–2543) on High Street has fifty-two rooms. Pets are allowed, and rates are very reasonable. The **Eagle's Lodge** (207–667–3311) on Bar Harbor Road does not allow pets, but it offers very affordable rates.

The **Ellsworth Comfort Inn** (207–667–1345) on High Street welcomes pets and offers very affordable prices. Sixty-some rooms and other nice amenities attract many families.

Most of the many other motels, inns, and B&Bs in the area are happy to have your children as guests. Among these are **Mrs. Bancroft's Bed & Breakfast,** which doesn't offer anything fancy but welcomes your kids and posts very low rates. The house is at 30 Wood Street; the phone is (207) 667–4696. Campers should have a look at the **Branch Lake Camping Area** off Route 1A; it has fifty-five sites with electricity, water, and sewer.

ROGER'S FAVORITE ANNUAL EVENTS IN DOWN EAST MAINE

Native American Festival, Bar Harbor; 207–288–3519
Down East Stampede, Machias; 207–255–4402
International Festival, Calais; 207–454–2211
Winter Harbor Lobster Festival, Winter Harbor; 207–963–7658
Mount Desert Island Summer Craftfest, Bar Harbor;
    207–794–3543
World's Fastest Lobsterboat Races, Jonesport-Beals Island;
    207–497–2804
Machias Blueberry Festival, Machias; 207–255–3524
Wilton Blueberry Festival, Wilton; 207–645–3932
Arcady Music Festival, Bar Harbor; 207–288–2141
Houlton Potato Feast, Houlton; 207–532–4216

It has swimming and water views, and they allow children and pets. You get all of this for as little as $12 a night.

Hungry families will find an abundance of food establishments in Ellsworth. The **Cheese Man** (207–677–8887) at 89 Main Street offers sandwiches and salads. **China Hill** (207–667–5308) on Bar Harbor Road will fix you up with Chinese food in a fine-dining setting for reasonable rates. **Czy Gil's** (207–667–3621) on Route 1 has family dining at low rates.

The best subs in town might be found at the **Ellsworth Giant Sub** (207–667–5585) on Bar Harbor Road. **Pepino's Mexican Restaurant** (207–667–5842) on Bar Harbor Road can put some spice into your meal if you like Mexican cuisine. **The Mex** (207–667–4494) is another good choice for Mexican fare; it's at 185 Main Street. **Larry's Pastry Shop** (207–667–2557) at 241 East Main Street is a perfect place for pastry.

When you leave Ellsworth, you will want to be on Route 3, also known as Bar Harbor Road. Route 3 intersects with Route 102 near Thompson Island. If you stay on Route 3, you will wind up in Bar Harbor. If you go down Route 102, you will find yourself in Acadia National Park. Flip a coin—you can't lose in either direction. If you're at the intersection, you are on Mount Desert Island. Let's assume you are hungry, so we will go to Bar Harbor first.

BAR HARBOR

Famous since the 1800s, **Bar Harbor** is on **Mount Desert Island.** Named *L'Isles de Monts-Déserts* in 1604 by Samuel de Champlain, Maine's second-largest island provides plenty of natural recreation through its seventeen mountains and five large lakes. A bridge was built from the island to the mainland in 1836. Once access was easy, painters came to Bar Harbor to fill their canvases with images that were distributed far and wide. Soon Bar Harbor was a big hit with steamboat tourists, and then trains brought people from such cities as New York and Philadelphia. By 1880, Bar Harbor was growing by leaps and bounds as a summer resort. Today, the harbor area remains a major tourist interest.

The **Natural History Museum** (207–288–5015) at College of the Atlantic on Route 3 is a good place to stop with the kids. Hours are 9:00 A.M. to 5:00 P.M., daily, from mid-June to Labor Day and 10:00 A.M. to 4:00 P.M. September to May. Children can see numerous species of wildlife represented in the museum. The animals are mounted, as are skeletons of local species. Sea tanks show off the local marine life, and there is usually a special activity planned for the kids. Admission is $2.50 for adults and 50 cents for children.

If your kids are interested in lobster farming, take them to the **Oceanarium Lobster Hatchery** (207–244–7330) at One Harbor Place, West Street. The hatchery is open six days a week from 9:00 A.M. to 5:00 P.M. June to late October is the season for this facility. You and your children will witness the daily routine of a working lobster hatchery, where thousands of lobsters are being farmed for future release. Admission is $3.95 for adults and $2.75 for children.

Whale watching is a favorite Maine activity, but before you go out on a boat, visit the **Bar Harbor Whale Museum** (207–288–2025) at 52

Acadia National Park should be on your list of family adventure destinations. (Courtesy Maine Office of Tourism)

West Street. This is a fabulous place to learn about whales. Best of all, admission is free, but donations are accepted.

Native Americans used Mount Desert Island for living, hunting, and fishing. Their activities are memorialized in the **Robert Abbe Museum at Sieur de Monts Spring** (207–288–4532). Signs will lead you from Route 3, south of the Jackson Laboratory, to the facility. This place offers fascinating exhibits. Children will be enthralled here. They will probably love the authentic tepee and birch-bark canoe, as well as the jewelry, moccasins, baskets, and other artifacts on display. Dioramas show the living conditions of the region's Native Americans throughout the changing seasons. Exhibits change periodically to reflect recent archaeological excavations. Adults pay only $2.00 for admission; kids pay $.50. This is a bargain and an educational experience all in one. While you're here, step out to the adjacent **Wild Gardens of Acadia,** an easy stroll among some 300 species of native plants labeled and displayed along a self-guided trail. The museum and gardens are open from May to October from 10:00 A.M. to 4:00 P.M., except in

July and August when the hours are extended to 9:00 A.M. to 5:00 P.M.

Bicycles are a favored mode of transportation around the island. If you would like to rent some two-wheel transportation, contact **Acadia Outfitters** (207–288–8118) at 106 Cottage Street. They are open late May through September; 8:00 A.M. to 8:00 P.M. **Bar Harbor Bicycle Shop** (207–288–3886) at 141 Cottage Street is another rental option. They are open 8:00 A.M. to 8:00 P.M. seven days a week in season, and 10:00 A.M. to 5:30 P.M. Monday through Saturday in the off-season. The **Acadia Bike & Canoe Company** (207–288–9605) at 48 Cottage Street rents all kinds of bikes plus trailers for young children. Open 9:00 A.M. to 6:00 P.M. Tuesday through Saturday in the spring and 9:00 A.M. to 6:00 P.M. seven days a week in summer. If you want a guided bike tour, check out **Cadillac Mountain Bike Adventures** (207–288–4532) at 110 Main Street. They provide sunrise breakfast rides from **Cadillac Mountain,** lakeside lunches, and sunset dinners.

Tennis players can use the courts at **Atlantic Oakes by the Sea** (207–288–5801) on Route 3 to keep in form. Golfers have the **Kebo Valley Golf Club** (207–288–3000) to keep themselves busy. Located on Eagle Lake Road, this eighteen-hole course has been seeing divots for over 100 years. Younger golfers will enjoy **Pirate's Cove Adventure Golf** (207–288–2133), about 4 miles north of Bar Harbor on Route 3 at **Salisbury Cove.** This course is open from 9:00 A.M. to 11:00 P.M. daily. Three acres of fun are here in this miniature golf extravaganza. Picnic tables and snack bar help make an afternoon or evening here pleasurable.

How about communing with harbor seals and taking a walk around a salt marsh? You can do this at the **Oceanarium Bar Harbor** (207–244–7330), about 4 miles north of the national park entrance on Route 3. Kids love to get close to the seals and watch them play at feeding time. You can also take a fisherman-led tour of the connected Maine Lobster Museum and a guided trip around a salt marsh. The place is open Monday through Saturday from mid-May through early October. Admission is $6.00 for adults and $4.50 for children (includes lobster hatchery).

Nature lovers can't resist **Downeast Nature Tours** (207–288–8128). You can tour by bike, foot, or cross-country skis to see bald eagles, osprey, other fauna and flora, and exciting natural features of the land and sea. Tours are offered in half-day and full-day packages. Overnight camping tours can be arranged. They are open year-round and tours leave sunrise to sunset. Prices are $10 per hour per person. A half-day package is $40. Special group rates can be negotiated.

Fitness fanatics can flock to **Lotus Gym & Lotus Organic Natural Foods Cafe** (207–288–5598) at 16 Mount Desert Street. This full-featured gym has weight facilities, stair-climbers, and more than two dozen multi-station trainers. You can participate in low- and high-impact aerobics. Private showers, whirlpools, Karate, and free orientation to the equipment are just some of what is offered. Healthy foods and drinks are sold on the premises. There is something here for almost anyone. The cafe is open 10:00 A.M. to 7:00 P.M. Monday through Friday, 12:00 to 3:00 P.M. Saturday, and closed on Sunday.

Arrange an outing with the **National Park Tours** operation by calling (207–288–0300). Tickets are available at Testa's, Bayside Landing, 53 Main Street. Tours start at 10:00 A.M. and 2:00 P.M. You will ride a bus for about two and a half hours through some of the most beautiful country in the world. It's my understanding that this outfit has been satisfying customers for over four decades. Reservations are highly recommended.

Rock climbing is a popular sport in Acadia National Park. You don't have to be an expert or even have any previous experience to enjoy an introduction to scaling granite cliffs. **Atlantic Climbing** (207–288–2521) at 24 Cottage Street will be happy to show you and your children what rock climbing is all about. Small, personalized courses are offered for all age and experience levels. You can choose half-day adventures that expose you to real climbs in Acadia or more advanced treks of several days. Instructors are professional guides with years of experience.

Another reputable rock-climbing outfitter is **Acadia Mountain Guides** (207–288–8186). Here you get professional instruction for climbing even if you have never before found a foothold in rock. All safety equipment is provided, and you can arrange half-day, full-day, or many-day experiences. This company is located at 137 Cottage Street at the corner of Route 3 and is open 8:00 A.M. to 8:00 P.M. mid-May through early October and 9:00 A.M. to 6:00 P.M. October through mid-May.

How long has it been since you rode a trolley? **Acadia National Park Tours** (207–288–3327) will take you on a one-hour tour of old mansions and of the mountains. Part of your trip will have you walking *on,* but not *to,* the summit of Cadillac Mountain, the highest peak in Acadia. This is an open-air ride, and the air, even in summer, can have a bite to it. Wear warm clothes and bring a jacket. Tours operate from April through August. You can buy affordable tickets at Testa's, Bayside Landing, 53 Main Street.

If you prefer, you can contact **Acadia & Island Tours** (207–288–9899) for a trolley ride. They also offer bus tours. Tickets are available at **Acadia Restaurant** (62 Main Street) or aboard the trolley. Tours run from May through October.

One of the most popular activities in Bar Harbor and its immediate environs is looking at the water and playing at its edges. Looking at the water is easy in this island community; it can be done almost anywhere. Playing at its edges is best done along the **Shore Path,** which starts at **Agamont Park** near the Bar Harbor Town Pier and is approximately 1-mile long and runs along the bay. This trail is also accessible from Grant Park, off Albert Meadow, at the corner of Main and Mount Desert Streets. Next to this, boat excursions rank high on the list of activities. Many boating experiences and water-related opportunities are just waiting for you. Just remember that the water is inviting but cold. The following operations offer some of the best choices in Bar Harbor for families.

If your kids are old enough and you have an adventuresome spirit, you can go out in a sea kayak. **Acadia Bike & Canoe** (207–288–9605) will fix you up with all the equipment needed and provide a Registered Maine Guide to lead your outing. These trips last anywhere from half a day to a full day; romantic sunset trips are also offered. All you have to do is show up at 48 Cottage Street and say you are ready to go. The company is open 9:00 A.M. to 6:00 P.M. Sunday through Saturday during summer and Tuesday through Saturday during spring.

Another outfit that will put you to sea in a kayak is **Acadia Outfitters** (207–288–8118) at 106 Cottage Street. Everything you need is included in the cost, and the rates are reasonable. The company is open 8:00 A.M. to 8:00 P.M. from late May through September. Reservations are recommended.

If paddling through salty water is a bit much for you and your family, consider riding on the *Acadian.* The **Acadian Nature Cruise,** offered by **Frenchman Bay Boat Cruises** (207–288–3322) at 1 West Street, Harbor Place, next to the town pier, sails daily from May to November. With a little luck, you will see seals, eagles, and porpoises off the coast. Other attractions may include lighthouses, islands, and gorgeous sunsets.

There is almost no end to the list of providers of water entertainment in Bar Harbor. **Bar Harbor Whale Watch Company** (207–288–2386) is at the Bluenose Ferry Terminal, 1 mile north of Bar Harbor on Route 3. Sailing from 10:00 A.M. to 4:00 P.M. May through October, you can ride this catamaran at 30 miles per hour in search of whales. The passenger list can number 140, all in a heated cabin. Free parking is provided during the trip.

The **Whale Watcher** (207–288–3322) at 1 West Street, Harbor Place, next to the town pier, is a 105-foot vessel. You should see humpback, fin, and minke whales as you ride smoothly over the ocean on this large ship. You are almost certain to get a sighting, and fringe benefits include dolphins, porpoises, and seals, not to mention sea birds. Parking is no problem, and there is even limo service from many resort locations.

Sea Bird Watcher Company (207–288–2025) has a 72-foot vessel waiting to take you to see anything from whales to puffins. Get your tickets at 52 West Street. If you want a slow, peaceful ride through the waters of Bar Harbor and surrounding areas, check out the **Chippewa Lighthouse & Islands Cruise** (207–288–4585) at the **Bar Harbor Inn Pier.** This family-style cruise will show you lighthouses and wildlife along the way.

How about a boat trip to Canada? The **Bluenose Ferry** (888–249–7245) goes from Bar Harbor to Yarmouth, Nova Scotia. This six-hour cruise is a round trip to Canada and back to Bar Harbor. Activities on board include buffet dining, bars, slot machines, duty-free shopping, and a kid's play area. The ferry sails from June to October. You can hook up with this fun-filled pleasure at 121 Eden Street. The cruise leaves at 8:00 A.M. and returns at 9:30 P.M.

For people who prefer a bird's-eye-view, **Island Soaring Glider Rides** (207–667–SOAR) at Bar Harbor Airport on Route 3 are exciting. Their literature says they offer fun for all ages, and each glider can carry two passengers. If you're into air travel, this might be worth a look. They are open 10:00 A.M. to sunset seven days a week from late May to

October.

When you are ready to eat, your only problem will be deciding where to go. Bar Harbor has no shortage of fine food. The following suggestions only scratch the surface of the eateries and restaurants that offer good choices and values for families.

The **Fish House Grill** (207–288–3070) at the intersection of Route 3 and Mount Desert Street is a very family-oriented restaurant. There's abundant parking, and the prices are affordable. It's open seven days a week for breakfast and dinner. Seafood, chicken, and steak are part of the dinner menu, as is a special children's menu. The food is superb.

If you like vegetarian dishes, stop in at the **124 Cottage Street Restaurant** (207–288–4383). If you haven't guessed, it's located at 124 Cottage Street. This place is also popular for its seafood, steak, and chicken dishes. Desserts here are heavenly. Call ahead for reservations to be sure you get a seat. Eat from 5:00 P.M. to closing.

If you are looking for something unique, investigate the **Cafe Bluefish** (207–288–3696) at 122 Cottage Street. Cajun-crusted salmon, West African chicken, vegetarian meals, and Greek pastries are part of the menu.

For a full family adventure, you can eat at the **Cottage Street Bakery & Deli Cafe** (207–288–3010) at 59 Cottage Street. All three meals are served. Gourmet pizza, burgers, salads, pancakes, sandwiches, and so forth are all sure to please the most discriminating tastes. They are open 6:30 A.M. to 10:00 P.M. May 15 to October 15.

If you've just finished a game of miniature golf at Pirate's Cove, stop into the nearby **Log Cabin Restaurant** (207–288–3910) on Route 3. Seafood and prime rib are the specialties. This family-style eatery has plenty of parking and is open seven days a week from 7:00 A.M. to 9:00 P.M., late May to October.

Want some Asian cuisine? The **Oriental Restaurant 2** (207–288–2236) at 191 Main Street can fulfill your desire. A children's menu and outdoor seating are available. No MSG or any other artificial flavors or enhancers are used here.

Testa's (207–288–3327) at Bayside Landing on Main and Cottage Streets is another good place to settle in for a meal. Italian dishes, seafood, and steak are the specialties. Harbor views, good service, and plenty of good entrees are offered here. You can also buy tickets for the Acadia National Park tours and boat rides here.

Epi Sub & Pizza (207–288–5853) at 8 Cottage Street is a favorite among children. There's not a lot of atmosphere here, but the food and prices can't be beat. Crabmeat rolls, pasta, quiche, pizza, and hearty salads are just some of what you may order. Hours are 10:00 A.M. to 8:00 P.M.

Still here and still hungry? Hit **Miguel's Mexican Restaurant** (207–288–5117) at 51 Rodick Street. It serves some of the best Mexican food to be found Down East. They open at 5:00 P.M. Wednesday through Sunday. The **Island Chowder House,** (207–288–5117) at 38 Cottage Street is tops when it comes to chowder, and the **Fisherman's Landing** (207–288–4632) at 35 West Street will fix you up with anything from hot dogs to boiled lobster.

Just as there are a host of good places to eat in Bar Harbor, so are there many magnificent places to spend the night. Considering all the fun, food, and entertainment in the region, you may plan to spend a few nights in town. Where will you stay? It's easy to find information on the more expensive lodgings and resorts in Bar Harbor, but you'll have to look harder for moderately priced and inexpensive accommodations. The following choices are especially affordable and welcoming to families.

The **Eden Village Motel and Cottages** (207–288–4670), about ten minutes north of the harbor on Route 3, offers rooms from less than $50 and cottages that run about $400 a week.

The **Wonder View Inn** (207–288–3358) at 50 Eden Street is another place that has some affordable rooms. Pets and children are both welcome here. This seventy-nine-unit motel on fourteen acres overlooking **Frenchman Bay** has extensive and nicely landscaped grounds for strolls, plus a swimming pool and dining facilities. Rates run from as little as $55 to as high as $120.

Other nice, not-so-expensive places that welcome children include the **Ledgelawn Inn** (207–288–4596) at 66 Mount Desert Street, **Thornhedge Inn** (207–288–5398) at 47 Mount Desert Street, **Bass Cottage in the Field** (207–288–3705) just off Main Street, **McKay Lodging** (207– 288–3531) at 243 Main Street, and the **Holbrook House Inn** (207–288–4970) at 74 Mount Desert Street.

Camping in the Bar Harbor region is an affordable way to extend your stay. **Blackwoods Campground** (207–288–3274) is located in Acadia National Park off Route 3, 5 miles south of Bar Harbor. You can camp here at any time during the year, and you will be close to Bar Harbor. If you want to make reservations, and you probably should, call (800) 365–2267 about eight weeks in advance. If you are camping between June 15 and September 15, reservations are recommended. Campsites cost between $8.00 and $16.00 a night depending on the time of year. Camping is free from the end of November through early April. The **Seawall Campground** (207–244–3600), located on Route 102A, 4 miles south of Southwest Harbor, is open from late May to late September. Campsites cost $14 a night. This is a first-come-first-served campground where reservations cannot be made. The campground is very busy during late July and August. If you don't get there early, you may end up waiting in line. There are many other campgrounds in the Bar Harbor area, so bring your gear and spend some time under the stars.

After you're settled in Bar Harbor, you are within easy driving distance of a number of fun activities. If you backtrack a bit along Route 3, you'll reach the **Acadia Zoo** (207–667–3244) in Trenton. It is a wonderful place to take your children, and it makes a great day trip once you are booked into your lodgings in Bar Harbor. The zoo is open daily from 9:30 A.M. to sunset from May to November. Some forty-five species are housed on the fifteen-acre enclosure. Some of what you can see are native Maine species, such as whitetail deer, foxes, porcupines, and moose. Exotic wildlife is also here to see and photograph. Leopards, reindeer, and monkeys lead the list of those. Bison, wolves, cougars, camels, and domesticated animals like goats and donkeys round out the list of other species here. Birds are also plentiful and colorful. Unlike any other place in Maine, you can visit an indoor rain forest exhibit here. It features mammals, reptiles, amphibians, and birds of the rain forest. Most children are drawn to the zoo's petting area, which allows them to watch and touch such domestic animals as goats, rabbits, and sheep. Admission for adults is $5.00; children are charged $4.00; toddlers under three are admitted free.

Trenton is also a good place to find recreation of a more civilized nature. **Odyssey Park** (207–989–7670) on Route 3 is something of an amusement park—something you don't see a lot of in Down East Maine. Your kids can play on speed boats, aqua bikes, go-carts, bumper boats, and a variety of kiddie rides.

Airplane rides can be arranged at the Trenton airport at **Acadia Air** (207–667–5534) on Route 3. They will rent aircrafts, give flight instructions, or take you on a sight-seeing or whale-watching expedition. They are open seven days a week 7:00 A.M. to 7:00 P.M. in April, 7:00 A.M. to 9:00 P.M. May through October, and 7:00 A.M. to 6:00 P.M. November through March. You can play eighteen holes of golf on the **Bar Harbor Golf Course** (207–667–7505) at Route 3 and Route 204 in Trenton. Once you are finished bouncing around in Trenton, you can head into Acadia.

ACADIA

The acreage now known as **Acadia National Park** came under the protection of a public land trust formed in 1901 through the efforts of the island's wealthiest summer residents, among them Charles W. Eliot, then president of Harvard University. This group of citizens was greatly assisted by its director, George Door, who spent his fortune and energy taking control of some 11,000 acres for the park. By designating the area as protected space, portable sawmills were kept out of the property and overdevelopment was controlled. By 1916 Door had convinced the federal government to give the trust national monument status and later, in 1919, to officially establish it as a national park, the first such park east of the Mississippi. Presently, Acadia National Park accounts for about one-half of the entire island, consuming some 40,000 acres. Statistics indicate that about five million people set foot in the park each year. Most of them never see the finer points that you and your family can enjoy in relative peace and seclusion.

Hiking is a favorite activity within the park, as is rock climbing. You can take an easy, 3⅓-mile walk around **Jordan Pond Loop Trail,** or you can opt for a more vigorous climb along the **Precipice Trail.** While less than 2 miles in length, this trail is very steep and in some places uses iron rungs as ladders. Strenuous even for experienced hikers, this trail is not recommended for young children. Consult a ranger for advice. The park has many other wonderful hikes appropriate for families.

Summers are rarely brutal in Maine, but it can get hot. Ocean water in this area can be as cool as fifty degrees, which is pretty cold by the standards of most people. If you want to swim, consider some of the nice lakes and ponds which will be much warmer. **Sand Beach,** about 4 miles south of Bar Harbor, offers supervised swimming. **Echo Lake,** 11 miles to the west of Bar Harbor, is also a good, supervised swimming area. **Seal Harbor,** on Route 3, provides a town beach with parking and good swimming. **Lake Wood** is one of the warmer swimming holes. It is perfect for children, but there are no lifeguards on duty. To get to the lake, turn off Route 3 at the Cove Motel and take the second left, which is a dirt road. A small sign points the way to the lake. There is good parking and a short walk to the water.

The national park has a visitor center at the Hulls Cove entrance near the start of the Park Loop Road. It is open from May through October, and you can contact it by calling (207) 288–5262. Main headquarters are at Eagle Lake on Route 233 (207–288–3338). If you prefer to write for information, you can do so with the following address: Superintendent, P. O. Box 177, Bar Harbor, Maine 04609.

The park is full of magnificent views, clean air, and excellent trails. Industrialist and philanthropist John D. Rockefeller, Jr. donated more than 50 miles of single-lane, gravel carriage roads that provide cyclists, equestrians, joggers, and hikers access to some of the park's prettiest acreage. Cross-country skiing is popular on the carriage roads in winter. Seventeen stone bridges connect the roadways. These trails put you in touch with remote nature without interference from motorized traffic.

The 27-mile **Park Loop Road** is also a prime tourist trail, but it is open to automobiles. A four-day pass for using the road will cost you $10. Hikers and bikers are charged $3.00 for a four-day pass. It would be a bargain at twice its price.

Other towns you might want to visit before leaving the island include **Southwest Harbor** and **Bass Harbor.** Southwest Harbor is home to **Mount Desert Oceanarium** (207–244–7330), on Clark Point Road, where you can see many exhibits and displays of sealife, including about twenty tanks filled with marine creatures. One of these is a touch tank where kids may pick up crabs, snails, and other interesting species. The **Causeway Golf Club** (207–244–3780) in Southwest Harbor is a nine-hole course with pull carts and a pro shop.

Sand Beach offers a warmer swimming option for those not used to Maine's ocean.
(Courtesy Maine Office of Tourism)

Ship Harbor on Route 102A near Bass Harbor is a great nature trail to take a stroll along. The **Bass Harbor Head Light** is a lighthouse that you may want to photograph. You can take ferries out of Bass Harbor to visit **Swans Island** or **Long Island,** if you are so inclined.

With all of this exploration behind you, it's time to go farther Down East. Once you leave Acadia National Park and the Bar Harbor area, there are no more big-name places to go Down East. This is not to say that there are no attractions and activities—it's just that they are scattered out and not as well known. This can be good. You may not have to share your Maine adventure with as many other tourists in these areas.

The down side of moving out of a well-known tourist area is that you have to drive a bit more to reach special places and attractions. On the plus side, you will find fewer crowds and see more of what Maine life is really like. How far you go and how frequently you meander down country roads is up to you. There are, however, plenty of good sights in Down East Maine.

U.S. Route 1 is the coastal route, the artery to Down East. To get back to this road from Mount Desert Island, all you have to do is retrace the steps that took you to the island. You will take Route 3 from the Trenton area back to Ellsworth. Here you will pick up Route 1 and then Route 184, which you will take to Lamoine Beach.

LAMOINE BEACH

Lamoine Beach is a small, out-of-the-way place basically at the end of Route 184. The kind of beach where you are likely to find more area residents than tourists, it is a very good salt-water swimming beach with more than 2,700 yards of beach frontage.

Just a stone's throw from the beach is **Lamoine State Park** (207–667–4778), another well-kept secret on Route 184. Open from mid-May to mid-October, this 55-acre park is often ignored, but it shouldn't be. Picnicking is always in season here, and the pebble beach is fun to walk on. Kids can always enjoy skipping a few flat rocks on the water. Campsites in the park number in excess of fifty. Often available when no other campgrounds have vacancies, many of these sites have water views. You will also enjoy spectacular views of Cadillac Mountain. There is a boat launch and a dock on which to sit and watch the sun set. You can also fish and hike here. This park is only about 11 miles from Acadia's Hull Cove Visitor's Center, so it's not a long haul from other scenic sites. If there is any disadvantage to this campground, it is that it does not have hot showers.

When you've explored Lamoine, get back to Route 1 and continue your trek to the farther reaches of Down East. You might want to sidetrack to little towns like **Winter Harbor, Milbridge,** and **Jonesport,** which are all worth a look. Most of what they offer are scenery and relaxation, but sometimes that is all it takes to have a good time. When you are in Washington County there are a number of small towns that offer some form of entertainment.

STEUBEN

Steuben is a little town on Route 1 that offers some superb hiking opportunities. **Petit Manan National Wildlife Refuge** is 6 miles off Route 1 on Pigeon Hill Road. A 5-mile trail here will take you around woods and coastline. Pine trees, cedar bogs, marshes, and blueberry fields provide habitat for many species of birds. Get out your binoculars and cameras for this walk.

MILBRIDGE

Milbridge is another Route 1 town that greets you along the coast. **McClellan Park** is here, overlooking **Narraguagus Bay.** Picnic tables, fireplaces, campsites, and restrooms at this park make it a great place for families.

If you're happy just meandering in Down East, you have a choice in Milbridge. Staying on Route 1 will take you to **Cherryfield,** which is somewhat inland. Driving up Route 1A will keep you along the water and guide you to **Harrington.** Once you pass through Harrington, which you will do on either Route 1 or Route 1A, you will arrive in **Columbia Falls.** Route 1A returns to being Route 1 in Harrington.

If you want a bite to eat in Milbridge before you make the decision, stop by the **Milbridge House** (207–546–2020) on Main Street. This family-owned restaurant opens at 10:30 A.M. and closes at 8:00 P.M. April through November. The menu is varied, and the prices are geared to families. If for nothing else, stop in for a piece of pie that you will not soon forget. Another good place to take the kids is **The Red Barn** (207–546–7721), also on Main Street. Pasta, steak, chicken, and seafood are some of what you can choose here. The kids may enjoy selections from the children's menu. They are open 7:00 A.M. to 9:00 P.M. and prices range from inexpensive to moderate.

JONESPORT

A detour from Route 1 onto Route 187 will take you into **Jonesport** and to the bridge to nearby **Beals Island.** Both of these are lobstering villages with a flair unique to Maine. **Great Wass Island** is also accessible by bridge from Jonesport. Never judge a book by its cover. Jonesport is deceiving. The village may seem small at first, but further investigation will reveal antique shops, restaurants, a picture-perfect marina, and many more shops and lodging facilities. Lobsters are big business in Jonesport, but don't overlook the crabmeat—it's delicious.

Captain Barna Norton (207–497–5933) has been offering bird-watching cruises to **Machias Seal Island** since the 1940s. He and his son run a good ship, and the island is a preferred nesting spot for puffins in June and July. These colorful birds pose perfectly for shutterbugs. Razor-bill auks and arctic terns take over the island in August and September.

Tootsie's Bed and Breakfast (207–497–5414) was the first B&B in Washington County. To this day, it is still one of the finest. Don't get me wrong—it's not fancy or exotic and only two guest rooms are available, but it is very clean and very inexpensive. A room and a hearty breakfast can be yours for $25 to $40. Pets are sometimes allowed.

Jonesport "By The Sea" (207–497–2590) at 1 Main Street is another good choice. Five guest rooms are here, and they cost $45 to $65 a night. If you are camping, try your luck at **Henry Point Campground** on the Kelly Point Road off Route 187. This place is open from April through November, but no showers, laundry facilities, or drinking water are on site. If you want to shower or cook, don't plan on doing it here. If you just need a place to pitch your tent for the night, however, this pretty campground is surrounded by salt water on three sides.

For breakfast, lunch, or early dinner, the **Tall Barney** on Main Street is open from 7:00 A.M. to 7:00 P.M. It's not much to look at, but the food will make you glad you chose to grab a booth or stool. You are likely to see many Mainers as you enjoy your meal at this local gathering place. Lobstermen favor the restaurant, as do tourists, and prices here will not burst your budget.

ROGER'S FAVORITE FAMILY ADVENTURES IN DOWN EAST MAINE

Robert Abbe Museum, Sieur de Monts Spring; 207–288–3519
Harbor Whale Watch Company, Bar Harbor; 207–288–2386
Acadia Zoo, Trenton; 207–667–3244
Odyssey Park, Trenton; 207–667–5841
Acadia National Park, Acadia; 207–288–3338
Lamoine State Park, Lamoine Beach; 207–667–4778
Oceanarium Bar Harbor, Bar Harbor; 207–288–5005
National Park Tours, Bar Harbor; 207–288–0300
The Natural History Museum, Bar Harbor; 207–288–5015
Oceanarium Lobster Hatchery, Bar Harbor; 207–288–2334

BEALS AND GREAT WASS ISLANDS

If you venture across the bridges to the islands, check out the **Beals Island Regional Shellfish Hatchery** (207–497–5769). Open from May through November from 9:00 A.M. to 4:00 P.M., this is a good place for your children to get a lesson in marine management and sea life.

After you've explored Beals Island, head over the Green Bridge to Great Wass Island. Walking trails are **Great Wass Island**'s claim to fame. More than 1,500 acres are combined to create this piece of land. Many parents choose a short, 2-mile trail along the shore to **Little Cape Point** to hike and picnic. Kids love to scamper over the smooth rocks and look for hidden treasures. There are coastal peatlands to see, as well as Maine's largest jack-pine stands.

After a long walk, some ice cream might hit the spot. Visit **The Islander** (207–497–2000) on Alleys Bay Road from 3:00 to 9:00 P.M. for some soft ice cream. You can get fried clams if you prefer.

There is one motel on Great Wass Island. You can call **Rose Marie's Motel** at (207) 497–2511 to make reservations. Rates range from $35 a night to $400 a month. Camping is not encouraged on the island.

JONESBORO

Head back over to the mainland on Route 187 to **Jonesboro,** the last major town before you get to Machias. There is not a lot of fluff to this town, but the scenery is hard to beat. Situated along the **Chandler River** and **Chandler Bay,** you are never far from water when driving around Jonesboro.

Roque Bluffs State Park is about 6 miles out of Jonesboro on what else but Roque Bluffs Road. When you are close to the park, you take a right turn on Evergreen Point Road to get to the swimming area. Once in the park you can choose between a salt-water pebble beach and a sand beach on fresh water. The sand beach is easier to walk on, and the water here is always warmer than on the pebble beach. Hard sea breezes can be cold even in late summer on the pebble beach. Kids love the playground in the park, and parents like to relax at the many tables provided in the area. You will find diaper-changing facilities, grills, and rustic toilets to meet your other needs.

The **Blueberry Patch Inn** (207–434–5411) on Route 1 is a fine place for you and your family to spend the night. Each unit has a refrigerator, television, air conditioning, and phone, and a pool is on the premises. Room rates are $30 to $45.

Right next door to the inn is the **Whitehouse Restaurant** (207–434–2792), which opens before most people's eyes do at 5:00 A.M. and closes at 8:00 P.M. You can sit in a booth or opt for counter service. The staff is as friendly as can be, and the seafood is the choice of most patrons. Prices aren't bad.

MACHIAS

The Machias River runs through Machias, offering good salmon fishing from mid-May through early June. This town has a lot of history pertaining to patriots during the American Revolution. **The Burnham Tavern** (207–255–4432) is an educational stop. Open 9:00 A.M. to 5:00 P.M. Monday through Friday from June to Columbus Day, this 1770s tavern is filled with period furnishings, and it tells the story of how locals captured the British man-of-war, *Margaretta,* on June 12, 1775. When the local townspeople went out in *Unity,* a small sloop, to stop *Margaretta,* they triggered the first naval battle of the Revolution. Admission is $2.00 for adults and 25 cents for children.

Machias was once second only to Bangor as a lumber port. Now, it is famous for the **Maine Wild Blueberry Company,** which is said to process about 250,000 pounds of blueberries a day. Yes, I did say a day. This makes it the world's largest processor of wild blueberries.

If flying makes you hungry, you can rest assured that you won't leave Machias with an empty stomach. **Graham's Restaurant** (207–255–3351) at 3 East Main Street is open all year and serves three meals a day from 5:00 A.M. to 8:30 P.M. It's a laid-back place until dinner, when the ambience and service become a bit more formal. Prices are moderate. **Helen's Restaurant** (207–255–8423) at 32 Main Street caters to big groups, but this is not to say that you and your family are not welcome. By all means, stop in. Sandwiches, seafood, various meats, and salads are all on the menu. Pies and other desserts are raved about here. Prices are affordable.

MACHIASPORT

Not far from Machias on Route 92 is **Machiasport. Fort O'Brien** is also here, but it is mostly just a mound of earth that was used as an ammunition dump during the American Revolution and the War of 1812. A more entertaining place in Machiasport is **Jasper Beach.** This is a pebble beach that is rich in colored stones. If you continue down Machias Road through Machiasport, you will run out of land at **Starboard,** which is a beach with incredible views. This little route is full of water views and down-home Maine living.

LUBEC

When you leave East Machias on Route 1 you might consider taking a right turn on Route 189 when you get to Whiting. This road will take you to **Lubec,** right on the edge of Canada, and to the bridge from Lubec to **Campobello Island** in Canada. Once a center of the sardine industry with twenty sardine-canning plants, Lubec still houses two active plants.

The **West Quoddy Light State Park** on South Lubec Road is open from mid-April through October from sunrise to sunset. Since this is the easternmost tip of the United States, it is the place to be if you want to be the first in the country to see a sunrise. A lighthouse decked out with red and white stripes is on the property. It dates back to 1858 and is still operating. There are beaches here, but the water is cold. A 2-mile trail leads you along the cliffs to **Carrying Place Cove,** but due to dangerous heights, this is not a good hike for young kids. Certainly, this is a pleasant place to take a break from driving.

Another possibility for fun in Lubec is the **Sunrise Air-Lubec** (207–733–2124) adventures. You can go up for scenic views, fish watching, and aerial photography.

Lodging in Lubec includes **Christies of South Bay** (207–733–2599). You can bring your children and your pets to this friendly establishment. Three guest rooms with shared baths can be booked for less than $60 each per night. **The Home Port Inn** (207–733–2077) at 45 Main Street offers seven guest rooms from $80 per night. **The Peacock House** (207–733–2403) at 27 Summer Street is an old 1880s house. Five guest rooms, one of which is accessible to the physically challenged, await you. Rates range from $55 to $80.

The Hillside Restaurant (207–733–4223) on Route 189 would be the first to admit that it's not fancy and doesn't have a view worth writing home about. They let their delicious dishes do their talking. Chowder and lobster salad sandwiches are local favorites. They're closed on Tuesday and don't open until 11:00 A.M. on other days. Not a bad place to satisfy your appetite without emptying your wallet.

Once you have explored Down East, you can head north to the wild North Woods for wilderness at its best. You won't find a lot of fast-food places or fancy hotels, but the region is rich in rewards for those who love nature and solitude.

Northern Maine

Northern Maine is a big piece of real estate. Most of the land is wild and undeveloped. While you won't find theme parks and amusement parks in the north woods, you and your children can find plenty of wholesome family fun. This section of Maine is not for people who need arcades and bustling shopping malls to enjoy themselves, but neither do you need to be an expert in wilderness survival to get the most out of the area that I think is one of Maine's best attributes.

Camping is an economical way to see the north country, but rental cabins, cottages, and motel rooms are plentiful around key areas. You don't need four-wheel drive to reach most of the remote areas, as the roads provided for logging trucks are quite passable by car.

BANGOR

Bangor is a pretty large town, by Maine standards—in fact, it's Maine's second largest city and the gateway to the north woods. Easily reached from I-95, this old logging town has become quite a place for business interests. **Bangor International Airport** (207–947–0384), for instance, is served by all major airlines and handles jet traffic from all over the world. The city even boasts a large mall (appropriately named the **Bangor Mall**) that houses some eighty stores. It is on Hogan Road, just west of exit 49 from Interstate 95. If you're heading north, the mall may offer your last taste of major civilization.

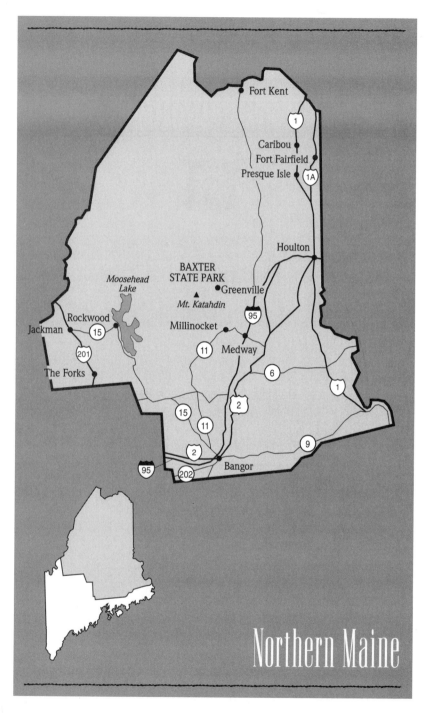

Northern Maine

Children's activities are limited in the north country, but Bangor does provide museums, fishing opportunities, golfing, and shopping. While you're in Bangor, consider a shopping trip to **The Briar Patch** (207–941–0255) at West Market Square at 29 Broad Street. Open from 10:00 A.M. to 5:00 P.M., this large store features children's books and toys. Also at 1 West Market Square is **The Grasshopper Shop** (207–945–3132), which carries toys, clothing, jewelry, and gifts. This store is open 9:00 A.M. to 6:00 P.M. Monday through Saturday, until 8:30 P.M. on Thursday, and 9:30 A.M. to 5:30 P.M. on Sunday.

You might want something to read when you head north to camps or cabins. Bookstores in Bangor include **Bett's Bookstore** (207–947–7052) at 26 Main Street, **Mr. Paperback** (207–942–6494) at Main Square, **BookMarc's** (207–942–3206) at 78 Harlow Street, and **The Booksource** (207–941–0255) at Crossroads Plaza.

When your shopping bags are full, rest your weary feet at the ol' fishin' hole. A favorite local spot is the **Bangor Salmon Pool,** located about 2 miles south of the city on Route 9, off North Main Street in Brewer. This pool collects Atlantic salmon as they are making their runs upstream. If your legs *haven't* given out, the **Bangor Municipal Golf Course** (207–945–9226) on Webster Avenue offers eighteen holes. Aficionados of vehicles of all kinds may enjoy the **Cole Land Transportation Museum** (405 Perry Road; 207–990–3600), which displays such land rovers as old-time wagons, snowplows, trucks, sleds, and rail equipment. This collection exhibits some interesting models and provides a good history lesson. The museum opens May 1 and continues to operate until early November. Hours are 9:00 A.M. to 5:00 P.M. daily. Adults are charged $2.00 for admission; kids get in free if they are under eighteen years of age.

If you plan to stay in Bangor for the night, consider making reservations at the **Hamstead Farm** (Fuller Road; 207–848–3749), the perfect accommodations for families who have rarely or never had the chance to spend time on a farm. Open throughout the year, Hamstead Farm offers lodging in an 1840s farmhouse. Three guest rooms, one with a private bath, await weary travelers. Your children will thrill at the opportunity to see a variety of farm animals, including turkeys, cows, pigs—maybe even a bunch of kittens. A double room will cost you about $50 and includes a good, old-fashioned farm breakfast. This type of place is not for everyone, but it is a good place for families who'd love to walk off the car cramps on the 150 acres surrounding the farmhouse.

If you're looking for a good, quick place to eat as you move north, try the **Governor's Take Out and Eat In** (207–947–3113) at 643 Broadway in downtown Bangor. The place opens early for breakfast and stays open late for dinner. Hamburgers and steaks are on the menu, as is German potato soup and fresh strawberry pie and ice cream. Hours are 6:00 A.M. to midnight.

Miller's Restaurant (427 Main Street; 207–942–6361) is another good dining option. They offer a great buffet with many meal choices and it includes making your own sundaes. Prices are family friendly. They're open Monday through Saturday 11:00 A.M. to 10:00 P.M. and Sunday 10:30 A.M. to 8:00 P.M.

Once you leave Bangor you can go in any direction, of course, but many travelers head north on Interstate 95. Most visitors get off Interstate 95 at Medway and begin their glorious expedition of the north woods while remaining in some semblance of civilization.

MEDWAY

Medway is no metropolis, but you can have lots of fun here. If you like to fish, you can find excellent waters for smallmouth bass in this area. Kids can swim and play along the sandy shore of a river that is open to the public. Float planes will take you for aerial tours, and campgrounds are close by. For fast food and other "normal" conveniences, you are going to have to go farther north to the town of Millinocket, but there's no real need to rush there. Medway is a great place to start your family adventure of the Maine woods.

By the time you get off the exit ramp at Medway, your kids may be looking for a place to let off some steam. A nice public access place just up Route 157 (the road you'll be on) has a small playground, a boat ramp, and a sandy beach on the east branch of the **Penobscot River.** The water is shallow at shore and grows deeper gradually. River currents are not a problem, even for small children who stay close to the beach. This is a great place to take a break. There's even a little country store on the right side of

ROGER'S FAVORITE ANNUAL EVENTS IN NORTHERN MAINE

Snowmobile Rally, Greenville; 207–695–2702

Moosemania, Greenville; 207–695–2702

Forest Heritage Days, Greenville; 207–695–2702

The International Seaplane Fly-In Weekend; 207–695–2702

The Ice-Out Contest, Greenville; 207–695–2702

Katahdin Family Bluegrass Music Festival,
    Medway; 207–723–4443

Haunted Trolley Ride, Millinocket; 207–723–4443

The Can Am Crown, Fort Kent; 207–834–5354

Maine Potato Blossom Festival, Aroostook; 207–532–6561

Northern Maine Fair, Presque Isle; 207–764–6561

the road at the intersection of Route 157 and Route 11, just before you get to the parking area for the river access.

After you pause at the store, you can either drive up Route 11, which parallels the river, and stop at any one of the pull-offs with picnic tables, or you can continue on Route 157 to the beach area. The latter choice is a good one if you have your fishing poles and want to wade the river for smallmouth bass. Campers and people who enjoy rustic cabins can stay at **Pine Grove Campground and Cottages** (Route 11; 207–746–5172) and enjoy riverfront accommodations. Fees are inexpensive, starting at $14.50 for a campsite for a family of four, and the campground has sites for tenting, RVs, and cabin dwellers. A small store is on the premises. The season here starts on May 20 and runs to September 30. Pets are allowed, and so is swimming in the calm river waters near the campground. This facility is suitable for children, but it's a little rough around the edges (older furnishings and rustic cabins).

If you choose to stay on Route 157, you will cross a bridge that spans the river and then turn right, into the beach and river access area. Don't be surprised to see a float plane near the boat ramp. This is a take-off and landing spot for bush pilots, but they don't endanger the swimming area. After getting refreshed here, continue on Route 157 to **Katahdin Shadows Campgrounds** (800–794–5267). Open year-round, this facility caters to tenters, RVers, and cabin dwellers. These very nice cabins have lofts, and they are kept spotless by the on-site owner and his staff. This campground is less than 2 miles from the exit off Interstate 95, on the right side of Route 157. A good sign points the way up a winding road to a virtual playground in the wilderness and in the shadow of Mount Katahdin. This is a premier spot for adults and children.

What makes this campground so special for kids? Dozens, if not hundreds, of soft, lovable bunny rabbits are a good start, and the clean, courteous conditions add to the list of benefits. An arcade, an outside pool, and an enjoyable playground produce favorable responses from children. This facility is well maintained and managed, so that children can go off on their own, within reason, and meet playmates and friends in safety. The owner of this campground is very active in its management, and he is tuned into the needs of parents and children.

You can use the Medway area as a base camp while exploring a variety of local activities. Canoeing, rafting, fishing, hiking, plane rides, and photo opportunities are the primary close-in attractions. If you stay at Katahdin Shadows Campground, the owner will assist you in making arrangements for trips by plane, canoe, or raft.

Once you leave Medway you'll want to head north on 95 toward Houlton where you'll pick up Route 1 and travel north to Presque Isle.

PRESQUE ISLE

Presque Isle is considered by many to be the heart of Aroostook County. This northern city provides a hub for people who live in the vast rural environment of Aroostook County, known locally as "The County." If the people of agricultural Aroostook County crave fast food, department stores, or a selection of new cars, they generally drive into Presque Isle. Caribou, a city about 11 miles out of Presque Isle, provides the only other option within miles for what most people consider creature comforts. The County is not known for it's lavish lifestyle. Residents in what is often called potatoland are wholesome, hardworking, down-to-earth people. If you are inclined to visit the working farmlands of the north, Presque Isle is one of your best choices as a home base.

Recreational themes in the Presque Isle region include swimming, playing tennis, skiing, golfing, snowmobiling, hunting, fishing, camping, and more. All of the normal accommodations for a routine life can be found in this remote city that is nestled along U.S. Route 1, about 50 miles outside of Houlton, where I–95 is left to venture into the farm country.

A big pull to the Presque Isle area is **Aroostook State Park** (207–768–8341), located at 87 State Park Road. The park is about 5 miles south of town, just off of Route 1. If you and your family enjoy camping, stop here where you will find thirty wooded sites with tables and fireplaces available for tents and camping trailers. To make camping reservations, call (207) 287–3824. Reservations can be made from June 15th through Labor Day.

Hikers will find comfortable trails within the park. The North Peak Trail covers 1.25 miles, starting at the day-use parking area. Magnificent views abound among the hardwoods and conifers. The North-South Peak Ridge Trail meanders along a ridge between two peaks for a distance of about 1 mile. South Peak Trail is short, less than 1 mile, but it is a rugged walk. The trail is steep and rocky. Other trails are also available within the park.

Are you up for a picnic? A lakeside picnic area offers tables, charcoal grills, a swimming area, and a place to change from street clothes to swimming suits. You can launch your own boat or canoe, or you can rent a canoe, along with needed accessories, to explore the pristine waters within the park. Whether you have a day or a week to spend, The Aroostook State Park is an excellent choice for families.

If you're interested in the history of Presque Isle, visit the **Presque Isle Historical Society** (207–762–1151), at 16 Third Street. The society was founded in 1963 to collect items of interest that illustrate life in the Presque Isle region. The **Estey House Museum** offers public hours on Thursday from June 20 to September 5. Hours are from noon to 3:00 P.M.

Presque Isle doesn't offer numerous attractions for children, at least not in terms of amusement parks, beaches, or zoos. But, what you will find in this rural town is good people and a natural environment that is surrounded by modern conveniences. Consider Presque Isle as your jumping off point to Maine wilderness.

If you plan to stay overnight in the area, you might want to make reservations at the **Northern Lights Motel** (207–764–4441). It is located on Route 1, close to the park. The **Budget Traveler Motor Lodge** (207–769–0111), on the Houlton Road, houses sixty-two modern rooms, offers laundry facilities and kitchen units. Your pets are welcomed here. **Keddy's Motor Inn** (207–764–3321), also on the Houlton Road, has 151 rooms, a restaurant, lounge, and an indoor pool. Pets are accepted here, too. Need another option? Try the **Northeastland Hotel** (207–768–5321), on Main Street. Here you will find fifty-one rooms, a restaurant, and a lounge.

Would you prefer a camping experience? Contact **Arndt's Aroostook River Lodge and Campground** (207–764–8677), at 95 Parkhurst Siding Road. You and your family could make a vacation out of staying here, without a need for outside entertainment. You will enjoy swimming, biking, fishing, canoeing, and golfing on an adjacent golf course. There are tent sites and pull-throughs for big rigs. Views from most sites are spectacular.

Finding food in Presque Isle is not a problem. If you are in the mood for fast food, you can find everything from tacos to roast beef along the main drag through town. Most major food franchises are represented along this route. Sit-down dinners are also plentiful. If you like Polynesian, Chinese, and American cuisine under one roof, try the **Mai Tai** (207–764–4426), at 449 Main Street. More interested in a famous "Winnie's Burger?" Check out **Winnie's Restaurant and Dairy Bar** (207–769–4971), at 79 Parsons Street. **Vickie's Hometown Pizza** (207–762–6262), at 63 State Street, is an ideal place to indulge your Italian appetite. A short drive around town will show you over two dozen possibilities for meals.

When you've satisfied your Presque Isle appetite, hop back on Route 1 and head north to Caribou.

CARIBOU

Caribou is a small town in northern Maine that provides services to thousands of residents who live in surrounding rural areas. This town doesn't offer any glitz or glamour, but it does provide a variety of activities for families. Caribou is a favorite jumping off point for those interested in visiting Canada or seeing a different part of Maine. In contrast to the Maine coast, Caribou boasts of woods and fields. This part of Maine, and the surrounding towns, are developed around agricultural land. Potatoes are the crop of choice, and you are likely to see many more farm tractors than sports cars on the roads.

Most of Maine is appreciated as a tourist hotspot. Caribou doesn't fit this profile. When you venture into the deep north of Maine, you will find small communities that depend on each other more than they do on the out-of-state dollars that support much of Maine. Aroostook County, where Caribou is located, is a grassroots part of Maine that few tourists take the time to explore. If you want fancy restaurants and a bevy of shops to spend hours in, Caribou is the wrong place to go. However, if you want to see a working side of Maine that few people ever do, Aroostook County is an ideal place to put on your travel agenda.

To reach Caribou, you travel north on I–95 to Houlton. Once you arrive in Houlton, you will take U.S. Route 1 all the way into Caribou. It's very easy to find this overlooked part of Maine. If you are heading into Caribou from Presque Isle, you will have to drive only about 11 miles up Route 1. The roads are good, but farm tractors can slow you down. Be alert to the farm equipment in the area, drive slowly, and enjoy the scenery.

Funland Amusement Park (207–493–3157) is located about 3 miles south of Caribou on Route 1. This is one of the few attractions in Caribou that might remind you of the southern part of the state. What can you and your children do at Funland? Start with miniature golf. If you are up to a more adult version of golf, you can hit a bucket of balls at the on-site driving range. If you children prefer larger balls, they can spend time in the batting cages. A water slide is popular in warm weather, and there are go-karts for those with a desire to motor around the track. A game room offers calmer conditions, and kiddie rides are just right for your youngsters.

If you visit Caribou when there is snow on the ground, you might want to consider renting snowmobiles. This is an experience that you and your older children will not forget. **Earl's Snowsled Sales and Service, Inc.** (800–451–5281), at 595 New Sweden Road, will set you and your family up with top-quality snowmobiles to glide across the miles of groomed trails in the Caribou area. Open Monday through Friday from 9:00 A.M. to 5:30 P.M., and Saturday from 9:00 A.M. to 4:00 P.M., Earl's rents a two-passenger, new snowmobile at a rate of $100 for 24 hours. The first 150 miles of your trip is included in the rental rate. Additional miles are billed at a rate of 30 cents each. A $500 deposit is required at the time of rental and may be paid in cash or with a major credit card. During peak seasons, reservations are recommended.

There are a number of well-maintained trails for your riding enjoyment. Distances on the trails range from as little as 8 miles to more than 170 miles. It doesn't require much effort to take advantage of over 6,000 miles of groomed trails shared with Maine and Canada. Aroostook County offers you over 1,600 miles of prime trails, so you can ride until your heart is content.

Would you and your family like to go on a snowmobile tour? Call **Crystal Snowmobile Tours** (207–498–3220), or write to the company at P. O. Box 1448, Caribou, Maine, 04736. This company offers tours on more than 1,200 miles of groomed trails. Tour packages offer a number of options, including lodging, meals, snowmobiles, and guides. Call for precise pricing for the package of your preference.

If you've brought the family pet along and aren't sure where to leave him while you are out seeing the sights in wild, wonderful Caribou, not to worry, you can board your animals at **Home Farm Kennels** (207–498–8803). This facility is located on Old Washburn Road, and the mailing address is P. O. Box 813, Caribou, Maine 04736-0813. The kennel holds a state license and has been in business since 1976. Rates range from $5.00 to $8.00 per day. Many services are offered at various fees, you can call for exact details.

The Black Hill Kennel (207–496–3761), at RR 2, Box 4460, Old Limestone Road, is another option for the care of your little furry loved ones. Rates range from $4.50 per day for cats to $7.00 for dogs. Specialized personal attention for your pets is available in increments of 15 minutes, at a rate of $3.00 per session.

If you are looking for a cultural experience, visit the **Nylander Museum** (207–493–4209). It is located at 393 Main Street. Public hours for the museum in summer are Wednesday through Sunday, 1:00 to 5:00 P.M., Memorial Day through Labor Day. From March to May and from September to December, you can visit the facility from 1:00 to 5:00 P.M. on weekends.

Highlights of the museum include lifesize mounts of a bear and deer. You will see a mounted moose head, artifacts of early mankind, geological exhibits, butterfly and moth collections, and a section on marine life. An herb garden, at the rear of the facility, includes herbs once used by Native Americans and those introduced by early colonists. Over eighty herbs are represented.

You and your children can also revel in the view of over 40,000 shells that have been collected from all over the world. One of the finest collections of fossils in the eastern United States can be found in the small country town of Caribou. You would not normally expect to find such a fine facility in an out-of-the-way place, but the Nylander Museum makes it all available to you.

Caribou is located in a remote area of Maine, so you will likely want to spend a night or two in the hospitable town. This is not a problem, there are plenty of comfortable accommodations for you and your family to rest and reside in. Here are a few names and phone numbers to consider when you are seeking lodging.

The Riverside Motor Inn, (207–498–6071) at RR2, Box 4900 is a clean, affordable place for you and your family to spend a night or two. If you want something a bit more elegant, try the **Caribou Inn and Convention Center** (207–498–3733). It is located at the intersection of Route 1 and Route 164. There are seventy-three rooms, a restaurant, a lounge, a laundry, an indoor pool, and kitchen units available here. If you are planning an extended stay, this is a good place to make reservations. **The Days Inn** (207–492–3311), on the Access Highway is a good family option for lodging where your pets are welcomed. Facilities here include fifty-nine rooms, a restaurant, and a lounge. **The Old Iron Inn** (207–492–IRON) is a favorite bed and breakfast, located at 155 High Street. This is not a large facility, but you will get plenty of personal service with rates running from

$39–$49 for up to three people. Open throughout the year, you can enjoy a comfortable stay for fishing, snowmobiling, or just taking in the local sights.

There will come a time when food is on your mind. Just because you are in potatoland, there is no reason to do without fresh Maine lobster. Call ahead to **Yusef's Restaurant** (207–498–6454) and the chef will have your lobster dinner waiting for you when you arrive at 142 Bennett Drive. Craving an eggroll? Try the **Jade Palace Restaurant** (207–498–3648). It's located in the Skyway Plaza. When pizza strikes your fancy, it's hard to beat **Reno's Family Restaurant** (207–496–5331). Go to 217 Sweden Street and enjoy breakfast, lunch, or dinner at affordable family rates. **Frederick's Southside Restaurant** (207–498–3464) is another good choice. It is located at 217 South Main Street.

The time you spend in Caribou can be very special. There are not a lot of materialistic activities to partake of in this town, but if you enjoy seeing a slice of true Maine life, you can fulfill your dream in Caribou and surrounding areas. Natural activities, such as fishing, canoeing, hiking, and other back-to-the-earth elements can be found in this little-known haven in northern Maine.

Once you leave Caribou, head south on Route 1 to Route 95 South to Route 11/157 West and pass through **Millinocket** on Route 157, you are approaching Maine wilderness at its best. Route 157 becomes Route 11 in Millinocket. As you reach the outskirts of town, turn right on the **Golden Road.** This road is controlled by paper companies, and a small vehicle fee is charged for using it. The Golden Road is often busy with lumber trucks, and they have the right of way. This high-quality dirt road takes you on an unbelievable tour of the North Woods, and it grants you access to many recreational areas, such as Baxter State Park.

Baxter State Park (207–723–5140) is the centerpiece of this wonderfully wild place. The park is open from April through November and offers so many recreational activities that you should spend a few days to enjoy them. Camping is available, but reservations are essential. This park attracts a lot of visitors, so make camping plans early.

If you plan to tour the 200,000-acre park by car, allocate at least two hours for the trip and don't be surprised if it takes closer to three hours.

Mount Katahdin, Maine's highest mountain, affords beautiful views as well as extensive hiking trails. (Courtesy Maine Office of Tourism)

Mount Katahdin towers majestically over the area as Maine's highest mountain. You and your children will discover about 150 miles of hiking trails within Baxter State Park. The trails range in difficulty, but many are easy enough for small children to negotiate. Try the **Daicey Pond Nature Trail** if your kids are young. A free pamphlet on the trail is available from the ranger's station at **Daicey Pond Campground.** Call (207) 695–2702 or (207) 723–4443 for information.

Good swimming and canoeing can be enjoyed at **South Branch Pond,** where rental canoes are available. **Abol Pond** is another good swimming hole. If you and your family enjoy bird-watching, you will have an opportunity to see about 170 species in the park. Moose and deer can often be seen along the roads and ponds. Bears inhabit the area, but they rarely create a bother. Take precautions nonetheless—this park is pure wilderness. There is no running water for domestic use, no electricity, and no food or supplies in the park. You will, however, run into dense bug populations during summer months. Always bring insect repellent.

Let me give you a tip on black flies that I learned the hard way. On my first trip down the Golden Road I saw a moose. Being excited, I got out of my car and left the window rolled down to photograph the massive animal. After taking pictures and swatting flies and mosquitoes, I got back into the car. The tan headliner was black in spots with biting black flies. Keep your windows rolled up when you leave your car during bug season.

If you find yourself at the north entrance of Baxter State Park, you will be near the little town of **Patten.** The **Lumberman's Museum** (207–528–2650) is just ahead on Route 159. A working model of a sawmill is part of this museum. Other attractions include a blacksmith shop, old tractors, and thousands of artifacts from the logging industry. The facility is open from Memorial Day to September for regular hours of 9:00 A.M. to 4:00 P.M., Monday through Saturday and Sunday from 10:00 A.M. to 4:00 P.M. The museum stays open through October on weekends only.

If you come out of Baxter State Park the same way you went in, you will be back on the Golden Road. It will allow you to travel through miles and miles of unspoiled wilderness on your way west to the town of **Greenville.** You might want to stop at the numerous places along the way that are perfect for picnics and scenic photographs. You can find gas and country-store supplies along the Golden Road, as well as many sporting camps that offer places to stay for the night. Most of these camps are rustic, and many don't have electricity unless it is generated on the site, but basic amenities include beds, linens, gas lamps. Prices range from $45 to $100 a night.

Your trip down the Golden Road will parallel the West Branch of the Penobscot River. Excellent fishing is available in the river and area ponds. **Whitewater rafting** is another recreational option along this river. **North Country Rivers** (800–348–8871) is one of many outfitters in the area that can take you and your family down the river. The company rents wet suits for spring and fall trips. Children age ten and older can ride the lower section of the river, but passengers must be at least sixteen years of age to raft the Upper Gorge. The outfitter is open 8:45 A.M. to 5:00 P.M. seven days a week from late April to early October. The meeting place for rafting expeditions with this outfitter is the **Big Eddy Campground,** P.O. Box 548, Millinocket, Maine 04462.

This campground, which is near some of the finest landlocked salmon fishing in the world, is open to campers using both tents and RVs. Call (207) 723-9581 for more information.

Whitewater rapids are rated on a scale of one to six, with six being the most difficult. The rapids on this river range from three to five, with five being on the Upper Gorge. For a complete listing of licensed outfitters, you should contact the **Maine Department of Inland Fisheries and Wildlife** at (207) 289-2043.

A favorite view along the Golden Road is the **Ripogenus Dam.** Locals call it Rip Dam. The view over the gorge and along the river is outstanding. Be careful with young children in this area. The rocks can be slippery, and a fall into the river cannot be afforded and may, in fact, be deadly. After leaving the gorge, continue on the Golden Road until you come to **Greenville Road,** which will be on your left and marked by a sign. If you miss this turn, you will travel deeper into the wilderness, but there are few conveniences along the way. You will probably be ready to head for Greenville by this time, so keep your eyes open for the road.

Between Patton and Greenville, however, you will come to the town of **Kokadjo.** Just a few years ago this town boasted of a population of three. There were more moose than people. The settlement has grown a little, and the new population report indicates that the population is, "not many."

Kokadjo does have some modern dining facilities as well as a general store. The **Kokadjo Trading Post** (207-695-3993) is one of the eating options, and the **Northern Pride Lodge** (207-695-2890) is the other. Both are in sight of each other and offer good food at family prices. Both are open at 7:00 A.M. The Trading Post closes "when everybody leaves" and the Lodge closes at 11:00 P.M.

Northern Pride Lodge also offers rooms for overnight guests and campsites for tenters. The lodge is situated on **First Roach Pond.** Boats and canoes are available for rent, and the fishing is awfully good. Moose can be sighted from the road, and loons can be heard at night. Electricity is generated on site for the lodge. If you are looking for comfort and relaxation in the wilderness, this is a good place to stay. Rates are about $80 per night. (No children under 12 allowed in lodge, but welcome in campground.)

Kokadjo Camps (207–695–3993) can fix you up in rustic accommodations. Located next to the trading post, these facilities are along the **Roach River.** You can't beat the fishing, but it's fly-fishing only. Pets are allowed, but there is no electricity. Rates are $45 for two people, $11 for each additional person.

Once you leave Kokadjo, you're on your way to Greenville. As you approach the Greenville area, you will see **Lily Bay State Park** (207–695–2700) on your right. This 942-acre recreation area has a small beach on Moosehead Lake. There is a playground for your children, restrooms, and plenty of picnic spots. Canoe rentals are available, and there is a ramp to launch your own boat. Swimming is good, but the water can be pretty cold. There are campsites in the area. The park is open from May until the middle of October.

When you pull into Greenville, you may feel like you have just entered another world. After being in the remote North Woods, even a small town like Greenville looks impressive. This town has plenty of modern conveniences, but you won't find any elevators or skyscrapers. You are still way up north.

Moosehead Lake borders this town and is one of the big pulls for tourists. The lake is huge in surface area and very deep. It is Maine's largest lake, being about 40 miles long and up to 10 miles wide. The shoreline covers about 420 miles. Boats are available on a rental basis, but this is not a lake to explore on your own. Hire a licensed guide if you want to see the water. Due to the vast area and occasional high waves, the lake is dangerous for anyone who is not experienced with it. Unexpected waves can swamp a sixteen-foot boat in a blink of an eye. If you're up north in the winter, snowmobiling and ice fishing on the lake are very popular. Personally, I don't go out on ice, but lots of people do, and most of them come back safely.

One good way for you and your family to get a tour of Moosehead Lake without going to much trouble is to cruise on the **S.S.** *Katahdin* (207–695–2716), which calls Greenville home. *Kate,* as she is called locally, is a 1914 steam vessel that once played a key role in the logging industry. The boat that once hauled pulpwood now transports passengers

Beautiful Moosehead Lake offers a variety of recreational opportunities.
(Courtesy Maine Office of Tourism)

for a fee. A standard cruise takes about an hour and will show you the southern tip of Moosehead. Once a month, from June to September, you can arrange for the 80-mile Head of the Lake cruise. Another variation is the Mount Kineo cruise, which goes out to Mount Kineo Island. On standard rides, adults pay $12.00 and children (ages 5–12) pay $6.00. The boat is docked near Main Street in Greenville.

Other boat services on Moosehead Lake are the **Kineo Shuttle** (207–534–8812), which operates out of Rockwood, **Moosehead Water Taxi** (207–534–8847), and **The Wilderness Boat** (207–534–7305). All of these options for lake travel offer excursions. Call them for details like rates and schedules.

The Greenville area provides opportunities for golfing, fishing, hiking, moose watching, swimming, and horseback riding. Fine food and good lodging is also available in and around the town. You can even rent mountain bikes, from **North Woods Outfitters** (207–695–3288) on Main Street.

Colorful float planes dot Moosehead Lake around the town of Greenville. These planes are used to deliver mail, people, and supplies. They also play an important role in medical emergencies and in keeping an eye out for forest fires. You can hire a flying service to give you and your family an aerial tour. One of the oldest and best-known services on the lake is **Folsom's Air Service** (207–695–2821). Family-operated since 1946, this company can meet all of your backcountry flying needs. Other air services include **Currier's Flying Service** (207–695–2778) and **Jack's Flying Service** (207–695–3020), both of which offer excursion flights.

Horseback riding at **Rockies Golden Acres** (207–695–3229) in Greenville can take you up scenic trails for up to two hours at a time. Downhill skiing at the **Squaw Mountain Resort** (207–695–1000) is a popular winter sport for this region. If you have the courage, you can take a chair-lift ride here in the summertime for an outstanding view of Moosehead Lake. Cross-country skiing is also available throughout the region when the weather is right for it. For information call the chamber of commerce at (207) 695–2702.

If you're looking for a place to call home for a night or two, a variety of choices exist in the Greenville area. The **Greenville Inn** (207–695–2206) is located on Norris Street in Greenville. Open from April through November, this impressive place sits atop a hill with a commanding view of Moosehead Lake that will take your breath away. The inn's paneled interior walls of cherry, mahogany, and oak richly set off its fireplaces and a leaded-glass window, capturing a rustic yet elegant mood. Breakfast is included in your rate and the dining room of this inn is said to offer some of the best food in northwestern Maine. Rates run from about $85 for a room with a private bath to $90 for use of the carriage house (plus $15 for each additional person).

The Lodge at Moosehead (207–695–4400) was built in 1916 as a hunting lodge. Of its five guest rooms, four have lake views. Each room is decorated in a theme of its own; you might choose, for instance, the "trout room" or the "loon room." Your room will have cable television, a gas fireplace, a private bath, and a whirlpool tub. Rates are a bit pricey ($135–$185), but they include breakfast. If you want to splurge, this is a good place to do it.

The Greenwood Motel (800–477–4386) is an excellent choice for

ROGER'S FAVORITE FAMILY ADVENTURES IN NORTHERN MAINE

Baxter State Park, Millinocket; 207–723–5140
Daicey Pond Nature Trail, Millinocket; 207–695–2702
The Lumberman's Museum, Patten; 207–528–2650
Lily Bay State Park, Greenville; 207–695–2700
S.S. *Katahdin*, Greenville; 207–695–2716
Moosehead Resort and Ski Area, Greenville; 207–695–2272
Mount Kineo, Rockwood; 207–534–7362
The Birches Resort, Rockwood; 207–534–7305
Whitewater Rafting, Jackman; 207–668–4171
Squaw Mountain, Greenville; 207–695–2272

motel accommodations. Rates are affordable ($45–$60 for a double), and the service and facility are both good. Pets are allowed, and the rooms are air conditioned. Other area lodging facilities include: **Indian Hill Motel** (207–695–2623), **Chalet Moosehead Motel** (207–695–2950), **Kelly's Landing** (800–498–9800), and **Pleasant Street Inn** (207–695–3400).

When your tummy rumbles, you can choose to have pizza or other home-cooked specialties at **Auntie Em's** (207–695–2238) on Main Street, or you can have steak, ribs, or burgers at **Flatlander's** (207–695–3373) on Pritham Avenue. The **Greenville Inn** (207–695–2206) on Norris Street offers an upscale menu to inn guests as well as other diners, and home cooking is the specialty at **Kelly's Landing** (207–695–4438) at Greenville Junction. For something to brag about, try your luck at the **Road Kill Cafe** (207–695–2230) on the wharf at Greenville Junction.

When you have exhausted yourself in the Greenville area, head for the towns of **Rockwood** and **Jackman.** There's still plenty of beautiful scenery to be taken in. Route 16 (combined with Route 6) leads you out of Greenville on your way to a more westerly wilderness and to Rockwood.

Once you arrive in Rockwood, you will be greeted by **Mount Kineo,** which stands some 700 feet above Moosehead Lake. The entire mountain is made of green flint. Abenaki Indians used this flint to make arrowheads and tools. If you want a closer look at the mountain, take a ride on the *Socatean* (207–534–7362). This 48-foot, forty-five-passenger boat will cruise you around Mount Kineo and let you debark for lunch at the **Kineo House.** Lunch, cruise, and included gratuity costs $17 per person.

Unless you think that fishing, hiking, cruising, camping, and other basic outdoor country fun is not good for children, you'll find plenty to keep you busy in Rockwood. You might even want to stay a few days. Among the nice places to stay in the area is my favorite—**The Birches Resort** (207–534–7305). This family-oriented facility has much to offer. Nestled into groves of birch trees overlooking Mount Kineo, it is open all year, and the rates are moderate (about $76 for a double). The resort includes a large lodge with guestrooms, plus fifteen log cabins along the lake, some of which have floating docks. The cabins have one to three bedrooms and either Franklin stoves or fireplaces; a few are equipped with kitchens. Cabin tents (tents that offer as much room as a cabin) are situated here and there.

The lodge's dining room and the food served in it are out of this world. An outside hot tub and sauna will take the pain out of legs and backs that spent too much time on the trail. Windsurfing, sailboats, kayaks, canoes, fishing boats, and mountain bikes are available. Cross-country skiing is offered in winter. Pets are not allowed.

Another great place to stay is **Maynards in Maine** (207–534–7703), located on Route 6/15 on the **Moose River,** where, by the way, some great fishing can be found. This lodge was founded in 1919. About a dozen cabins are scattered around the grounds, and they have indoor plumbing. The current rate, per person, is around $48 a day; this includes three meals a day—two served in the dining room and one packed for the trail. The decor in the dining room is worth a visit, even if you don't spend the night.

When you leave Rockwood on Route 15 west, the next stop on your agenda should be the town of **Jackman,** in the area known as the Switzerland of Maine. The road you are on will intersect with Route 201. If you turn to the north, you can be in Canada in just a short time. Head south, and your Maine adventure continues.

Jackman is known as a frontier town. To this day, you may see a moose walking down Main Street. If the town feels to you like a jumping-off point to the wilderness, that's because it is. Jackman is the last civilized township before crossing the mountains into Canada. Bring some angling gear with you—the area boasts of some of the very best freshwater fishing in all of Maine. A famed canoe trip known as the **Moose River Bow Trip** covers 46 miles of the nearby waterways. Because it is long and somewhat arduous through some rough water, this type of trip is not good with young children, but it can be quite an adventure for teenagers. You can get more information on this and other Jackman activities by calling the chamber of commerce at (207) 668–4171.

If you head south down Route 201 toward **The Forks,** you are moving into whitewater country. The Forks is where the **Dead River** and the **Kennebec River** join forces. Many rafting and canoe companies ply their trade in this area. **Northern Outdoors, Inc.** (207–663–4466) is one of the largest, if not *the* largest, rafting outfitters on the Kennebec River. In conjunction with rafting, this company offers many other services. Its resort center, as it is called, at The Forks provides good food and entertainment. You can swim in a pool, soak in a hot tub, go fishing or mountain biking, and engage in stimulating conversation. Accommodations range from campsites for tenters to private cabins and condo-style environments. Rafting is the most popular activity here in warmer weather; skiing and snowmobiling provide the pull in winter.

New England Whitewater Center (800–766–7238) ranks right up there with Northern Outdoors, Inc. In addition to offering canoe trips, they operate the **Sterling Inn** in Caratunk. This building was a nineteenth-century stagecoach stop; it dates back to the early 1800s and now provides guest rooms for north-country travelers and canoeists. A few of the many other outfitters in the area are **Wilderness Expeditions** (207–534–2242), **Maine Whitewater** (207–672–4814), **Unicorn Rafting Expeditions** (207–725–2255), **Magic Falls Rafting** (800–207–7238), and **Moxie Outdoor Adventures** (207–663–2231).

While you are visiting The Forks, consider taking a short hike up to **Moxie Falls.** This 90-foot waterfall is said to be the tallest in New England. Turn onto Moxie Road from Route 201. The waterfall is on the south side of the bridge that crosses the Kennebec at The Forks. You can park off the road at the trailhead sign on your left. The hike is an easy one of less than a mile.

When you've had enough of the North Woods, you can come south on Route 201 to reach other areas of Maine. The scenery will change and so will the comforts—you are headed back into the modern world.

Central Maine

entral Maine is not filled with amusement parks, salt beaches, or mountains, but there is plenty of fun to be had throughout Maine, and the central portion is no exception. Take your time and enjoy the trip. Augusta is the state capital and offers a great museum for you to learn much about the state and the ways of life that have made Maine what it is today.

The Gray Animal Farm in Gray is a wonderful place to conclude your trek into Central Maine. You and your family can enjoy a picnic lunch while seeing wildlife that is indigenous to the state.

AUGUSTA

One of your first stops along Route 201 should be Augusta. Augusta is often called the heart of Maine. It is the capital city. Situated on the banks of the Kennebec River, Augusta has been a site of commerce since the 1600s, when a Pilgrim trading post was established within the city. This city has grown from housing a Pilgrim outpost to sporting the Civic Center, a host of business opportunities, and a quality of life that is hard to beat.

Augusta gained status as the capital city in 1827, seven years after the state of Maine was admitted to the Union. The mighty Kennebec River splits the city of Augusta, providing beauty and access. Located about 60 miles north of Portland and about 72 miles south of Bangor, Augusta is positioned in such a way to make it a hub of the state. Due to it's conve-

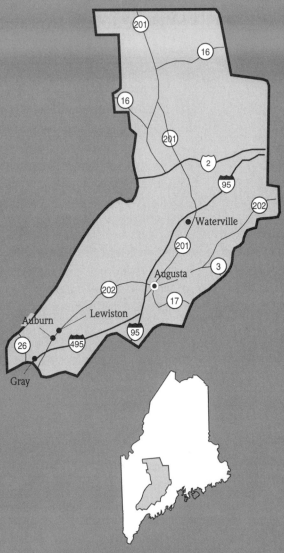

201

16

16

201

2

95

202

Waterville

201

Augusta

3

202

17

Auburn

Lewiston

26

495

95

Gray

Central Maine

The Maine State Capital Building is just one of the many interesting stops in Augusta.
(Courtesy Maine Office of Tourism)

nient location and airport, Augusta attracts the attention of businesses and residents in a way that few Maine cities enjoy.

How do you arrive in Augusta? I–95 provides easy access to the Capital City. Smaller towns, such as Hallowell and Gardiner, lie just outside of the main city and provide a variety of shopping experiences and historic lessons. Checking into comfortable accommodations in Augusta is sure to provide you and your family with a wealth of enjoyment opportunities.

The **Maine State Museum** (207–287–2301) is located in the Capital Complex, along Route 27. Look for the big dome of the State House, and you will have no problem finding the facility. This is the largest museum of history in the state of Maine. Exhibits in the museum reach back 12,000 years into the past. The facility is accessible to handicapped visitors, and wheelchairs are available on the premises. A gift shop is one of the first sights you will see, but what awaits you is incredible.

Hours of operation run seven days a week. The museum is open from 9:00 A.M. to 5:00 P.M. Monday through Friday. Saturday hours are 10:00 A.M.

ROGER'S FAVORITE ANNUAL EVENTS IN CENTRAL MAINE

Winter Carnival/Snowmobile Festival, Caribou,
    February; (207–498–6156)
17th Annual Northern Maine Agri-Business Trade Fair,
    Presque Isle, March 21–23; (207–472–3802)
Maine Sportsman Show, Augusta, March 28–30;
    (207–882–7032)
Lion's Home & Garden & Recreation Show, Augusta, April 5–7;
    (207–622–1539)
Kora Temple Shrine Circus, Lewiston/Auburn, April 18–19;
    (207–782–6831)
8th Annual Maine Mineral Symposium, Augusta, May 2–4;
    (207–657–3732)
14th Annual Maine State Parade, Lewiston/Auburn, May 3;
    (207–784–0599)
Great Falls Canoe Race, Lewiston/Auburn, June 14;
    (207–783–2249)
Antique/classic car show and golf tournament, stock car racing,
    and Caribou Homecoming Weekend, Caribou, July;
    (207–498–6156)
Le Festival de la Bastille, Augusta; July 11–13, (207–623–8211)
Bates Dance Festival, Lewiston/Auburn, July 26;
    (207–786–6077)
Festival de Joie, Lewiston/Auburn, July 31; (207–782–6231)
Northern Maine Fair, Presque Isle, August 1–9;
    (207–762–0071)
Caribou Cares About Kids, Caribou, August 15–17;
    (207–498–6156)

5th Annual Great Falls Balloon Festival, Lewiston/Auburn,
    August 22–24, (207–782–8964)
Rockhounders Rock & Mineral Show, Augusta, August 23–24;
    (207–873–6270)
Sidewalk Art Show, Augusta, August 30; (207–623–3781)
Crown of Maine Expo, Presque Isle, September 19–21;
    (207–764–6561)
Two-day arts and crafts festival, Caribou, October;
    (207–498–6156)
Harvest Arts & Crafts Show, Presque Isle, October 4–6;
    (207–764–6561)
Fall Craft Fair, Presque Isle, October 12–13; (207–764–6561)
The Festival of Lights, Caribou, December; (207–498–6156)
Holiday Light Parade, Presque Isle, December 7;
    (207–764–6561)

to 4:00 P.M. Sunday will find the doors open from 1:00 to 4:00 P.M. The museum is not extremely large, but it does pack a lot of punch in a small package.

What can you expect to experience within the walls of history? A diverse arrangement of exhibits awaits your inspection. A gem collection is intriguing. Old cars attract a lot of attention. The history of Maine's lumber work is a major topic, as is the procedure used to take ice from Maine's lakes and rivers. Marine life and the fishing industry is represented well in the museum. A personal favorite of mine and my children's is the natural history section, where you will find life-size mounts of many of Maine's animals. Even the textile industry is shown in a real-world environment. You and your family can spend hours investigating all of the interesting exhibits and still have time to visit the Children's Discovery Museum.

The Children's Discovery Museum (207–622–2209) is located at 265 Water Street, across from Key Plaza. This museum is built around a hands-on approach for children to learn from and have fun with. The bulk of the exhibits are for younger children, up through grade five in school. Children will be allowed to partake in real-life scenarios, such as a diner, a grocery store, and a post office. Children can take part in workshops, arts, crafts, family festivals, birthday parties, and environmental issues. Hours of operation vary, so you should call for current schedules and information. If your children are young enough to enjoy this type of activity, you should not miss the opportunity.

Old Fort Western (207–626–2385) is located on Cony Street, along the banks of the Kennebec River. This fort is Augusta's National Historic Landmark and New England's oldest surviving wooden fort building. It was constructed in 1754. The staff of the fort is costumed in eighteenth-century military, community, and family life regalia. Guided tours are offered during summer months. Hours and admission fees should be confirmed by calling the fort.

The Blaine House (207–287–2301) is located on the corner of State and Capitol Streets. Built in 1833, the Blaine House has been the official residence of Maine governors since 1919. Public tours are available Monday through Friday 2:00 to 4:00 P.M. Taking a tour of this house will enlighten your children to the ways of early architecture and show them a different type of Maine history.

The Civic Center (207–626–2405) is located in sight of the Augusta/Belgade exit of I–95. Accommodations for 7,000 people exist in the center's auditorium. In addition to the Paul G. Poulin Auditorium, the facility can accommodate 500 diners in the Augusta Room. Events at the Civic Center run from musical concerts to private meetings. Depending upon when you are in town, you may wish to check the schedule of events and consider spending some time at this major meeting place.

Now, what about places to stay? You will find numerous options in Augusta for lodging. **The Holiday Inn** (207–622–4751), at 110 Community Drive, next to the Civic Center, offers a fitness center, a restaurant, and a lounge at rates that will not ruin your vacation. If you prefer a Comfort Inn (207–623–1000) there is one at 281 Civic Center Drive. Here you

The Blaine House has been home to Maine governors since 1919.
(Courtesy Maine Office of Tourism)

will enjoy comfortable accommodations, a restaurant, a lounge, a health club, and an indoor swimming pool. **The Days Inn** (207–622–6371), at 390 Western Avenue, offers 128 rooms, an outdoor pool, free continental breakfast, and more, at affordable rates. Looking for a bit of luxury? Try **The Senator** (800–528–1234) at 284 Western Avenue. You can take advantage of luxury rooms and suites, award-winning dining, a fitness center, sauna, heated pool, hot tub, and nature trails for walking or jogging. Rates are a bit higher, but not as high as you might expect.

Augusta offers a smorgasbord of eating establishments. All the major fast-food places are represented, mostly along Western Avenue. If you have a hankering for Mexican food, try Margaritas (207–622–7874) at 390 Western Avenue. Opening at 4:00 P.M., they offer a happy hour from 4:00 to 7:00 P.M. and outstanding Mexican dishes. **Rebecca's West Side** (207–623–0021) will serve you breakfast, lunch, and buffets. You will find this fine eatery at 390 Western Avenue, the same address as Margaritas and Days Inn.

Ardito's (207–623–2044) at the Augusta State Airport, is a smoke-free, family restaurant specializing in traditional Italian food. **The Ground Round** (207–623–0022), at 110 Community Drive, is another fine family eatery. Looking for a hearty breakfast? Try the **Augusta House of Pancakes** (207–623–9775) at 100 Western Avenue. There is plenty of food sources in the greater Augusta area, and all of the establishments are easy to find. Plan to spend a day or two in Augusta, and enjoy yourself.

LEWISTON/AUBURN

After leaving Augusta by traveling south on Route 202, you'll come to the city of Auburn, which lies along the banks of the Androscoggin River. Only a bridge separates Auburn from its sister city of Lewiston. The Lewiston-Auburn area boasts the second largest population center in the state. The L/A area, as it is called by local residents is not rich in recreational activities within the city limits, but both cities are positioned to give travelers much opportunity in outlying areas that are not far away. For example, there are five major ski areas within two hours of the cities. The Oxford Plains Speedway is less than an hour away. Augusta, the capital city, is only a short drive up the Maine Turnpike, and L. L. Bean in Freeport is about thirty minutes away.

Lewiston's first official settlement was created in 1770. A single cabin was constructed by Paul Hidreth, of Dracut, Massachusetts, on the east side of the Androscoggin River. This was the beginning of a long and rich future for the twin cities. By 1795, the town was officially incorporated. The population grew to more than 1,000 residents by the year of 1810. In 1861, Lewiston was incorporated as a city, with a population in excess of 5,000.

The development of Auburn was not as simple as that of Lewiston. Auburn went through many name changes. The city began as Bakersville, changed to Poland, and then to Minot. Finally, in 1869, Auburn was chosen as a name that stuck and proved the test of time. At the time of its incorporation, Auburn was made up of settlements covering more than 66 square miles. This made Auburn one of the largest cities in the United States, when judged on the area of square miles.

Where the mighty Androscoggin River splits the two cities, there is a waterfall known as Great Falls. Water rushes down a drop of 54 feet and can be seen from the bridge that connects the two cities. Lewiston was first to harness the power of Great Falls. A long canal created for Lewiston was instrumental in propelling Lewiston ahead in the textile industry.

Auburn did not have the advantage of water power, so a different type of opportunity had to be created. In 1836 Auburn became home to the first organized shoe company in the state. The Minot Shoe Company was formed in West Auburn and took advantage of the railroad system. In 1865, approximately 600,000 pairs of shoes had been made. This number grew to an excess of six million by 1900.

Around 1905, a dam was built above the falls and provided Auburn with plenty of power. Within fifteen years, Auburn was the fifth largest shoe manufacturing center in the country. Growth was fast and good. Once the depression moved in, the sister cities suffered terribly and never fully recovered. The complexion of the cities changed, and continues to change, as an attempt is made to adapt to the new rigors of economical success.

What types of entertainment can you find in and around the L/A area? If you and your family enjoy lakeside picnics or dynamite bass fishing, **Lake Auburn** can fulfill your desires. This large, deep lake is located about 2 miles outside of Auburn, on Route 4. The water's surface covers more than 2,000 acres of prime fishing habitat. Bass and salmon are the two major attractions for anglers. Recreational boating is another main attraction to Lake Auburn, as is the public swimming offered at the outlet of the lake. Taylor Pond, near Young's Corner, is another spot where public swimming is allowed.

If you are in the Auburn area during snow season, you can enjoy some good skiing conditions at **Lost Valley Ski Area** (207–784–1561) P. O. Box 260, Auburn, Maine 04212 (off Young's Corner Road). Within about 2 miles of the city, you will find good slopes and one of the largest and best learn-to-ski schools in the state. You can ski day or night and take advantage of fifteen trails that range from beginner status to expert ratings. Everything you need to hit the slopes can be rented right on the site. There is also a cafeteria, a restaurant, and a lounge. Cross-country skiing is also available.

Municipal facilities for recreation are numerous. Basketball, softball, volleyball, soccer, track, aerobics, and weight training are offered from a variety of sources, such as local YMCAs and YWCAs. The Lewiston Multi-Purpose Center is another provider of recreational opportunities. There are close to thirty public tennis courts, twenty baseball fields, five outdoor hockey-skating rinks, five outdoor swimming pools, and several soccer fields. To gain complete information on these activities, you can call the local Chamber of Commerce at (207) 783–2249.

If you feel up to a little golf, either a driving range or a miniature course, you can check out **Taber's Driving Range & Miniature Golf** (207–784–2521), on Lake Shore Drive, in Auburn. Another driving range is the **College Street Driving Range** (207–786–7818), located at 601 College Street, in Lewiston. You can enjoy twenty-five tees with mats and artificial grass. Another twenty-five tees are available with grass tees. There are three target greens, a video training facility, a practice sand bunker, and golf supplies and repairs. There are even lights for after the sun goes down.

An indoor option to entertainment can be found at 729 Main Street, in Lewiston. You and your family can visit **Spare-Time Recreation** (207–786–2695) for some fun in any weather. How about some bowling? Candlepin bowling is offered at Auburn Lanes (207–783–3521). The lanes are located at 261 Main Street in Auburn.

If you need a place to board your pets while you are in the L/A area, you can call **The Animal Center** at (207) 225–2726. The kennel is located at R.R. 3, Box 630, in Auburn. Your pets will have a boarding kennel, pet supplies, and a veterinary hospital available.

Another option for fun can take you to new heights. You and your family can soar high above the twin cities and enjoy scenic flights that will leave lasting memories for years to come. If you are the adventuresome type, call **Twin Cities Air Services, Inc.** (207–782–3882) at the Auburn-Lewiston Airport in Auburn to investigate your aerial options.

For a more down-to earth adventure, you and your children can explore the 230 acres of the **Thorncrag Bird Sanctuary,** in Lewiston. This is one of the largest bird sanctuaries in New England, and it is located off Highland Springs Road. You will find Highland Springs Road on your left, off Route 126 (Sebattus Rd.) as you leave the city of Lewiston.

Let's talk now about places for you to rest and stay during your exploration of the Lewiston-Auburn area. **Super 8 Motel** (800–843–1991) at 1440 Lisbon Street in Lewiston offers non-smoking rooms with cable television, free local calls, king-sized beds, and recliners at affordable rates.

The Ramada (207–784–2331) at 490 Pleasant Street in Lewiston is another quality lodging facility. A sauna, whirlpool tub, heated pool, large suites, king-sized beds, cable television, and in-room movies are just a portion of what you can enjoy. There is on-site entertainment every night of the week, and the rates will not break your budget.

If you are looking for accommodations that are a little less fancy and on the outskirts of town, the **Redwood Motel** (207–784–5476) is a good choice. Located at 1986 Lisbon Road (Route 196), the Redwood Motel has an outdoor pool and clean, comfortable accommodations without a lot of frills. There is cable television, air conditioning, and a laundry room. The rates of this nice motel reflect a fairness of what you pay for what you get.

If you choose to spend a night in Auburn, you will find a restful night's sleep at **The Auburn Inn** (207–783–1454) at 1777 Washington Street. Rooms have been renovated recently and offer both smoking and non-smoking options. There is an outdoor pool for swimming, a full-service restaurant, a lounge, and entertainment.

Another Auburn option for sleeping arrangements is the **Coastline Inn** (800–470–9494) at 170 Center Street. You will get a free continental breakfast, free local phone calls, cable television, an option for non-smoking rooms, and free incoming faxes. Regardless of what side of the river you decide is best for your home base, you can find comfortable lodging in the L/A area without any problems.

You've had a busy day and found a nice place to spend the night, now you want some good food. **Mac's Grill** (207–783–6885) will serve you steaks or seafood in a friendly manner and at budget prices. This eatery is located at 1052 Minot Avenue, in Auburn. Pizza and donuts may seem like a strange combination, but don't knock it until you have tried **Georgio's Pizza & Donut Shop** (207–783–2981), at 740 Minot Avenue, in Auburn. Donuts are on the menu, but pizza is the specialty.

If you want a mix of steaks and Mexican food, you owe it to yourself to sit down at **Margaritas** (207–782–6036) at 838 Lisbon Street in Lewiston. **Luiggi's Pizzeria** (207–782–0701) at 63 Sabattus Street in Lewiston is an outstanding place for fabulous pizza. Open seven days a week, you can find fresh pizza here up until midnight from Sunday through Thursday and until 1:00 A.M. on Friday and Saturday nights.

TCBY Treats (207–784–3245) at 155 Center Street in Auburn, is an excellent place for frozen yogurt and hand-dipped ice cream. Cakes and pies are also available here. **The Heartland Restaurant** (207–784–3688) at the Promenade Mall on Lisbon Street in Lewiston is a wonderful place to take the kids. Chicken, steak, seafood, salads, and eighty-one dessert choices are just part of the menu. You will find service seven days a week. Kid's meals are available and served cheerfully. This is a true family-style restaurant.

Another great family restaurant is **The Ground Round** (207–784–1200) at 180 Center Street in Auburn. Your children will be thrilled by Bingo The Clown, and on Tuesday and Thursday, the meals your children consume cost no more than their weight at a rate of a penny a pound —what a deal! A full menu is offered until midnight every night. Steaks, barbecue ribs, chicken, salads, and fresh seafood are main entries on the menu. And, oh, don't overlook the free popcorn; your children will love it.

If you are in the mood for a more adult setting and are willing to drive for about twenty minutes, you can visit **Eli's Restaurant** (207–224–7090) at the Turner Highlands. Eli's is situated on a nine-hole golf course that is open to the public, so pack your clubs along with your appetite. Located on Route 117, in Turner, the Highlands Country Club and Eli's Restaurant has much to offer. The menu in the restaurant features char-roasted rack of lamb, grilled bacon-wrapped filet mignon, sea scallop saute, soups, salads, appetizers, and much, much more. This is an exceptional spot for you and your spouse to take a break from the routine kiddie meals.

When you are in the Lewiston-Auburn area, you are close to a wide variety of activities. Rates in the area are very affordable, and accommodations are comfortable and plentiful. The twin cities are well worth a long look when you are touring the state of Maine.

GRAY

Just a short drive south of Auburn is Gray, a little, out-of-the-way town that anyone with kids who love animals should take the time to visit. Since this area is off the beaten path, not many tourists flood the area. They just don't know what they are missing. As you enter this quiet town, you can grab a hot dog or an ice cream cone on your way to the **Gray Animal Farm** on

Route 26, about 3 miles north of town. Open from mid-April until mid-November, the farm plans guided tours on Saturdays from 11:00 A.M. to 1:00 P.M. and wildlife programs on Sundays from 1:00 until 3:00 P.M. But you don't need to be here for either of these structured events to have a great time. You and the kids are free to roam about any day of their operating season. Call (207) 657–4977 for information.

When you enter the game farm, you're driving down a paved drive with picnic tables under a pine canopy. Chain-link fence enclosures on both sides of the road behind the picnic areas reveal the presence of the farm's protected inhabitants. The first enclosures on your left house small animals such as coyotes, foxes, and skunks. The pens on your right are home to birds of all sorts, ranging from pheasants to vultures.

Once you park in the spacious grounds, you can venture off on foot. Don't forget to bring a camera or camcorder. As you pass a couple of buildings, you will come face to face with the white-tailed deer compound. A coin-operated vending machine filled with food provides you with the chance to have the deer eat out of your hand. If you walk to your left, you're entering bear country. Black bears are a Maine fixture, and you can see them here. A little farther down the path is the moose compound.

After chasing the kids back up the hill, stop at the bird pens for a breather. Turkeys may gobble at you, and pheasants are sure to strut their stuff. Crows may gawk, and peacocks will put on a show for your camera. Once rested, head down to the fish hatchery. If you've ever dreamed of big trout, this is a good place to see them live and in person. No fishing gear is allowed, but food is available for feeding the fish.

The paved paths are stroller-friendly, but some of the hills are a little steep. Access is good and easy for the most part. The animals here are essentially wards of the State, waiting to be reintroduced to the wild or living out their lives here in relative comfort. They get here by being injured or orphaned, and rehabilitators care for them in whatever way is necessary. This is not a roadside zoo designed to profit from passing tourists.

Our next destination is Western Maine, where you will find mountains, lakes, ponds, rivers, and—if you're lucky—maybe placer–gold. Yes, there is gold in them thar hills.

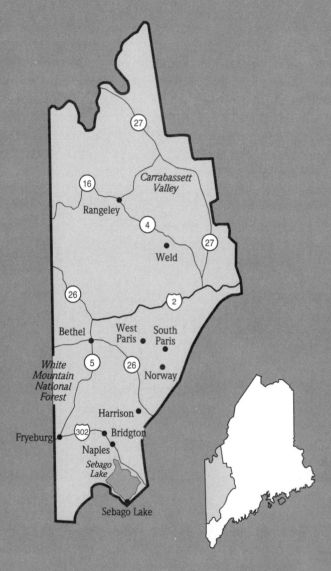

27

Carrabassett
Valley

16

Rangeley

4

27

Weld

26

2

Bethel

West
Paris

South
Paris

White
Mountain
National
Forest

5

26

Norway

Harrison

Fryeburg

302

Bridgton

Naples

Sebago
Lake

Sebago Lake

Western Maine

Western Maine

Western Maine is an area often overlooked by travelers. Many people concentrate their time in Maine along the coast or up in the North Woods, so they never see the state's western lakes and mountains. The beaches of Maine get most of the fanfare, so this is understandable. And, the wilderness areas up north promote a lot of tourism for hunting, fishing, rafting, and wildlife watching. Nevertheless, you shouldn't ignore the western part of the state. There is much to be seen along the way to Rangeley and Bethel, as well as a lot to do. Western Maine is something of a compromise for nature lovers and people seeking more modern excitement and activities. When you go west in Maine, you can have a lot of fun and still take in the beauty of unspoiled wilderness. While not as vast as the north country, western Maine offers plenty of outdoor activities while providing more fun for the kids.

SEBAGO LAKE REGION

The **Sebago Lake Region** is a good place to start your western adventure, and the medium-sized town of **North Windham** is as good a place as any to begin your tour. Located on Route 302, it offers all the conveniences that you are probably accustomed to. Fast-food restaurants and many attractions and activities line the roadside. North Windham has **Little Sebago Lake** to the north of it and **Sebago Lake** to the west of it. These lakes are a source of pleasure to both boaters and anglers.

Sebago Lake State Park (207–693–6613) is located just off Route 302 between South Casco and Naples. It is open from June 20 to Labor Day. Basically a day-use area, it offers beaches (with lifeguards), bath-houses, tables, grills, and, of course, water to swim in. A separate camp-ground has its own beach. There are, on occasion, guided tours along nature trails and presentations in an amphitheater. Camping is available.

NAPLES

As you move west on Route 302, you pass through the little town of Ray-mond en route to Naples. If you break off to the south on either Route 114 or Route 107, you will wind up in Sebago. For the moment, we will assume you are headed west on Route 302. When you reach Naples, you will see Long Lake and the Bay of Naples. The **Bay of Naples Camp-ground** (207–693–6429) is located here. Geared towards families, this campground offers 150 shady campsites, trailer hook-ups, a sandy beach, hot showers, laundry facilities, and a wide array of recreational activities. Your children can go swimming and fishing. Two playgrounds, ping-pong tables, pool tables, volleyball courts, horseshoe pits, badminton, and an adjoining public golf course are all available here. Hayrides, waterskiing, and boat and canoe rentals round out the list of activities.

Many people use the Naples area as their base camp for golfing (both regular and miniature), tennis, beaches, windsurfing, pap sailing, float-plane rides, and antiquing. Some folks visit the **Songo Locks,** which date back to 1830. This series of twenty-seven hand-operated locks once allowed people to come from Portland to Harrison. While the lock system is no longer used for this purpose, it does provide an excess of 40 miles of waterway for recreational boating.

The **Naples Historical Society Museum** (207–693–6790) at the Village Green on Route 302 will be of interest to history buffs. It's open in July and August from 10:00 A.M. to 3:00 P.M. and includes the old jail along with substantial memorabilia. If you are looking for something a bit more exciting, contact the **Naples Flying Service** (207–693–6591) for a 25-mile scenic flight over the Sebago–Long Lakes Area. Reservations are suggested and are accepted starting January 5. Para-sailing can be arranged by calling (207) 693–3888.

Canoeing on Sebago Lake is one of the many opportunities for family adventure in western Maine. (Courtesy Maine Office of Tourism)

One big attraction in the Naples area is the ***Songo River Queen II.*** This 90-foot sternwheeler river boat operates daily from July through Labor Day. Weekend excursions on the Songo River start in June and end in September. You and your family can enjoy a two-and-a-half-hour ride or a one-hour ride, depending upon your choice. Your destination will be the end of the river at **Brady Pond,** which you will reach through the only surviving lock from the 1830 canal that made up the Songo Locks. Mailboat rides on Songo Lake (207–693–6861 or 207–929–4705 in winter) are also available except on Sundays. This pontoon-style boat does not have toilet facilities and the ride lasts between one and two-and-a-half hours, so it may not be a good idea to take this trip with small children. The trips run from the last Saturday of June through the Saturday before Labor Day.

Golfers may wish to get acquainted with the **Naples Country Club** (207–693–6424) on Route 114. Tennis fanatics can turn to **Brady Pond Camps** (207–693–6333) on old Route 114. Horseback riding can be arranged at **Secret Acres Stables** (207–693–3441) on Lambs Mill Road, about 1 mile off Route 302.

Looking for something different? You don't have to go to Williamsburg, Virginia, to find people who know how to blow glass. Stroll into **Glassworks** on Route 114—about 3 miles off Route 302—and you will see everything from porcelain earrings to goblets and perfume bottles. You can visit the showroom and the studio. Watching the glassware being made is fascinating.

If the day's pleasures have exhausted you, look for accommodations at the **Inn at Long Lake** (Lake House Road; 207–693–6226), built in 1906. Its rates border on the expensive, but it offers special events, such as murder-mystery weekends. It's open from April through January. The **Augustus Bove House** (207–693–6365) doesn't allow smoking or alcohol, but a hearty breakfast is included in the $45 to $115 room rate.

BRIDGTON

If you choose to continue on Route 302, you will encounter the town of **Bridgton.** There are activities along Route 302 for children, but most of what you will find is aimed at older children and adults. The **Bridgton Historical Society Museum** (207–647–2765), for instance, has a collection that includes slides of the old, narrow-gauge railroad that used to run in these parts. The museum is located in the former fire station on Gibbs Avenue in Bridgton and is open from June to August from 1:00 to 4:00 P.M.

An eighteen-hole golf course is available at **Bridgton Highlands Country Club** (Highland Ridge Road; 207–647–3491), as are tennis courts. They are open from sunrise to sunset April to November. **Shawnee Peak** at **Pleasant Mountain** (207–647–8444) is reported to be Maine's oldest downhill ski area. It is on Route 302 in Bridgton and offers a vertical drop of 1,300 feet. About thirty trails operate here from December through March, and night skiing is available. The facility offers child care, equipment rentals, and lessons.

If you'd like a good place to take a dip and cool off during the hot weeks of Maine's summer, check out the little beach on **Long Lake** that the town of Bridgton maintains. It's a dandy. You will find it just off Main Street. Two other freshwater beaches in the area are **Woods Lake** on Route 117 and **Highland Lake** right on the edge of town. All are free, easy to find, and fun to take advantage of.

If you want to do a little shopping while you are in town, visit **Sportshaus** (61 Maine Street; 207–647–9528). It's open daily and offers a variety of apparel. While best known for its original Maine T-shirts, the store sells everything from casual clothes to skis and golf accessories. They are open 9:00 A.M. to 5:00 P.M. Friday and Saturday only. Maine artists display their wares at **Emphasis on Maine** at 36 Maine Street. Open daily, this shop displays the work of more than 700 New England artists and craftspeople. It's a treat to see.

You might want a bite to eat before you move on. Try the **Bridgton Lobster Pound** (207–647–8610) on Route 302. Don't let the name fool you. The kids can get burgers and hot dogs if they want to, and you can enjoy fresh Maine lobster at its best. Prices are moderate, and the atmosphere and service are above average.

FRYEBURG

When you are ready to depart from Bridgton, you may wish to go west to **Fryeburg** or south to **Sebago.** During most parts of the year your children will have more activities to enjoy in Sebago, but if you're here in the fall the **Fryeburg Fair** is big doings. In fact, it's Maine's largest agricultural fair. Held for a full week in October, it goes out with a bang on Columbus Day weekend. For information call (207) 935–3639.

If you go to Fryeburg in the summer, you should investigate the water fun at the **Saco River.** Water traffic can be quite heavy here due to the popularity of the river. According to the local outfitters, it's rated as the number-one canoeing river this side of the Mississippi. The sandy shores offer ideal picnic spots.

Saco River Canoe and Kayak (188 Maine Street; 207–935–2369) in Fryeburg will be happy to show you the river up close and personal. Shuttle service and canoe rentals are available. They are open 8:00 A.M. to 5:00 P.M. from May through October. **Saco Bound** (Route 302; 603–447–2177) is a New Hampshire–based outfitter, located just across the Maine–New Hampshire border, who will show you the Androscoggin River from May 3 through October 12. **Canal Bridge Canoes** (207–935–2605) in Fryeburg offers canoe rentals and shuttle services. If you have your own canoe, there are many places where you can put into the rivers on your own. Call (207) 935–3639 for information.

After a day on the river exploring the area's natural history, you might enjoy spending the night in a place with another sort of history. The **Admiral Peary House** (207–935–3365) at 9 Elm Street in Fryeburg is just the place to do it. This stately house was once home to Maine's famed Arctic explorer, Robert Edwin Peary. Now four large guest rooms with private baths and air conditioning await your arrival. A clay tennis court, a billiards room, and an outdoor spa are among the amenities here. Bicycles are also available. Rates are under $100 per night; full breakfast is included. Smoking is not allowed.

SEBAGO LAKE

Should you choose to turn south on Route 107 from Fryeburg toward Sebago, you will find more fun in the sun. **Douglas Mountain** provides you with a child-friendly hiking trail. It's a good way to burn off pent-up energy after your drive. This trail is on a Nature Conservancy preserve where terrific views of Sebago and the White Mountains can be taken in. Walking the trail should take less than thirty minutes, and the views are worth every minute of the easy climb. Once you reach the summit, you can venture down a short (less than a mile) nature trail. By car, you need to take Route 107 south from Sebago and turn right on Douglas Mountain Road. When you get to the end of that road, you will find limited parking and can begin your walk.

When you tire of walking, head down Route 107 and take a ride on one of the horses at **Sunny Brook Stables** (207–787–2905) in Sebago. The trail rides offered cater to both beginning and intermediate riders. The cost ranges from $15 to $18 an hour.

HARRISON

If you have decided to turn north out of Bridgton, Route 117 will take you to the town of **Harrison.** Harrison is a small town situated along the shores of Long Lake and Crystal Lake.

Harrison is home to **The Sheep Shop** at **Chardia Farm** (207–583–2996), a working farm, located at 1533 Maple Ridge Road, that sells wool and sheepskin products along with hand-spun yarn, shearling

ROGER'S FAVORITE FAMILY ADVENTURES IN WESTERN MAINE

Sebago Lake State Park, Sebago; 207–693–6613
Songo River Queen II, Songo River; 207–693–6861
Telemark Inn and Llama Farm, Bethal; 207–836–2703
Sunday River Ski Area, Bethal; 207–824–3000
Rangely Lake State Park, Rangely; 207–864–3858
Western Maine Children's Museum, Carrabasset Valley;
    207–235–2211
T.A.D. Dog Sled Services, Carrabasset Valley; 207–246–4461
Mount Blue State Park, Weld; 207–585–2347
Rangely Lakes Railroad, Phillips; 207–353–8382
The Stanley Museum, Kingfield; 207–265–2729

coats, vests, hats, and gloves. The kids may enjoy seeing the sheep, and the wool products can come in handy if you are in Maine during the winter months. The farm is open all summer, but by appointment only in winter months.

If you want to put up for the night, check into the **Tolman House Inn** (207–583–4445) on the Tolman Road. Open year-round, the inn is a former carriage barn with nine guest rooms with private baths in the building. Set on 100 acres of sloping hills, this facility includes a game room in the old icehouse, a dining area, and a lounge that overlooks spectacular gardens. Children under two stay for free, but you will need your own porta-crib. Rates, including breakfast, run from $60 to $75.

If you find the Tolman House Inn full, another good choice for lodging in the Harrison area is the **Snowbird Lodge** (207–583–2544). This is set on another 100-acre property that is lush with birch and pine trees.

Accommodations are basic and moderately priced. Amenities include a private pond, complete with beach, and a recreation room with a large, stone fireplace, a piano, television, VCR, and games.

Feeling hungry? Try the **Cracked Platter** (207–583–4708) on Maine Street in Harrison. You can't beat the hours—it opens at 6:00 A.M. and doesn't shut down until 1:00 A.M. Sundays are an exception, when the hours are 7:00 A.M. to 1:00 P.M. The menu is substantial. If you want it, they have it. Aunt Clara never made it any better. For down-home cooking at its best, stop into the Cracked Platter.

If you want a glimpse of Maine life from its most real perspective, however, riding the back roads of the western area will give you a view that few outsiders see. To the west of Harrison are the towns of Bethel and Rangeley, both of which are well known for their recreational areas. Northeast of Harrison are the towns of Norway, South Paris, and West Paris. They don't have a lot of flashy stuff to pull tourists in, but they do have some hidden nuggets of sorts. Want the insider scoop? Well, here it is.

NORWAY/SOUTH PARIS

If you are leaving from Harrison and want to check out some of the out-of-the-way areas of Maine, take Route 117 into Norway. There's a little picnic area and boat ramp right outside of Norway. This is not a trendy tourist place, so it shouldn't be too crowded if you decide to pull in here for a break from driving or a picnic lunch. When you come into Norway, you can either go toward **Oxford** on Route 26 or toward **South Paris** on Route 26. Fast-food places are available in this area but you can also check out **Sharer's Family Restaurant** (193 Main Street; 207–743–6367) and **Country Way Restaurant** (274 Main Street; 207–743–2387) for good food at reasonable prices. The main business district lies to the west on Route 26 between Norway and South Paris.

WEST PARIS

All of this part of Maine is known for its natural gem deposits. The town of West Paris is home to **Perham's Store** (Route 26, at the intersection of Route 219; 207–674–2341). This must-stop place is open daily from 9:00 A.M. to 5:00 P.M. What's in the store? Much more than you would imagine. Settle back, and I'll tell you.

The place to be for rockhounds, this gem, mineral, and rock shop was founded in 1919 by Stanley Perham. On the premises is a small museum, where admission is free for children and adults. Your children will get a first-class introduction to gems and minerals here. The impressive displays of the stones include some specimens of tourmaline, quartz, gold, and others in their rough, natural setting, some in finished form as jewelry, and even some that glow in the dark.

This is a store that welcomes the novice and satisfies the seasoned collector. You might say that no stone is left unturned! You can buy rock hammers, gold pans, chisels, lapidary equipment, and metal detectors. Rentals are available on some items, such as the metal detectors. Even if you have never had an interest in rocks, you will fall in love with this store. The polished stones and intricate carvings fascinate children and adults alike. And, it gets better.

Perham's has control of several quarries in the area. You can ask at the store for directions and search these areas without charge. What you find is yours to keep. Access is easy, and the rock piles are generally safe for even young children to poke around in. The only problem with Perham's is that there is so much neat stuff to buy that you will certainly leave wishing that you could have spent more money. Don't leave without purchasing at least one dish for gold panning. You'll be needing one when you arrive at the profitable banks of the Swift River (see page 144).

While you are at Perham's ask them to show you how to get to **Snow Falls Gorge.** It's right off of Route 26 in West Paris, but it's unmarked. You will find a waterfall that cascades into a gorge. Walk out on the bridge and enjoy the view. There are also hiking trails here.

BETHEL

The next stop on your tour of western Maine is the town of **Bethel,** but you will pass through the picturesque town of **Bryant Pond** along the way. The small town of **Locke Mills** will also be a landmark for you. Once you reach Bethel, still traveling on Route 26, you are in for some four-season fun. This town has a lot to offer—but it's not your average town. With a smaller population today than it had years ago, Bethel is best known now for the snow skiing in the area. Convenient to the popular tourist spot of North Conway, New Hampshire, Bethel's proximity to the White Mountain National Forest offers some of the best ski conditions in the East.

Popular in hiking seasons as well as in the ski season, Bethel is a quiet, down-home town that serves as a year-round stopping-over point for travelers going in many directions. Situated on the Androscoggin River, Bethel was once known as a farming and trading community, and it is still very much a working town. Lumber mills here produce pine clapboards, furniture parts, and a great number of broom handles. Yes—broom handles. In addition, I've heard that three local dairy farms ship some 7,000 gallons of milk a week out of the mountainous region.

What's in Bethel for *you?* Outstanding scenery is the first feature that comes to mind. White birch trees line the roads out of town. The river runs below the road, meandering through meadows and calling to anglers. Summer brings hikers and antiques buyers to the area, and winter, of course, draws skiers. The **Bethel Inn and Country Club** (1 Broad Street; 207–824–2175); pulls in golfers from far and wide. This eighteen-hole, championship-length course is challenging. The club's driving range allows you to tune up your short game and your driver. Clubs and golf carts are available for rent. The Inn is open all year, but the dining room is closed from April through November. The golf course operates from May through October.

Golf is not the only pull to this area. If you like to hike mountain trails, Bethel is one of the best places to do it. The **White Mountain National Forest** has most of its nearly 42,000 acres in New Hampshire, but enough of it stretches into Maine to provide ample entertainment for outdoor types. The local ranger can provide trail maps to anyone who requests them. Call (207) 824–2134 for maps and other information.

A short distance from Bethel is a place called Gilead, right on Route 2. If you turn left on Route 113 at Gilead, you will wind up in the national forest at the point where the **Wild River** and the **Androscoggin River** meet. Stop at one of the many pull-offs along Route 113 to fish, picnic, or wade in the shallows of the river. This really is a great place for kids to get a little break from riding. Wilderness campsites are farther down Route 113 in the forest. For information call (800) 280–2267.

Other hiking areas near Bethel include **Grafton Notch State Park** on Route 26 between Newry and Upton and **Screw Auger Falls,** about 1 mile past Grafton Notch. **Step Falls, Mother Walker Falls,** and **Moose Cave** are also in the region. If you would like some help along the trail, you should call **Telemark Inn and Llama Farm** (207–836–2703). Located 10 miles outside of Bethel on Kings Highway, this farm features llamas trained as pack animals that will accompany you and your family into the woods on guided tours from July through August. The folks at Telemark will arrange day trips or overnight camping trips of up to six days. The llamas carry the gear. If you arrange an overnight package, it can include meals, camping or lodging in the inn. Reservations are required. They are also open in the winter months as a private ski touring area. For more information visit them at their website at www.maineguide.com/bethel/telemark.

If you enjoyed Perham's Store in West Paris, you will probably like **Mt. Mann Jewelers** (207–824–3030) on Maine Street in Bethel. This gem and rock shop is not as extensive as Perham's, but it is well worth your time. You can gather a wealth of information here and buy some fine jewelry at the same time.

You can't say Bethel to Mainers without evoking their thoughts of skiing. Both cross-country and downhill skiing are possible in the area. **Sunday River Ski Touring Center** (207–824–2410) has plentiful, well-maintained trails that hold snow when other trails don't. The trails are open to the public and operate December through March. The center can give you Friday night guided night skiing, rentals on equipment, lessons, and snacks. The **Bethel Inn and Country Club** (207–824–2175) opens its golf course to cross-country skiers in the winter, creating trails throughout the course. **Carter's X-Country Center** (786 Intervale Road; 207–824–3880) has about 1,000 acres of cross-country trails open in season; some of these run along the Androscoggin River. Cabins are available, too.

Downhill skiing at **Sunday River Ski Area** (207–824–3000) is a big boom to Bethel in the winter. More than one hundred trails are here and are open until the snow melts. There is even a train that runs from Portland to Sunday River on the historic Grand Trunk Railroad route. A favored feature at Sunday River is the guarantee that you can learn to ski in just one day. There is even a SKIwee class for little youngsters between the ages of four and six. With strong snow-making ability and good grooming, this resort stays busy well into spring.

Mount Abram (207–875–5003) is not in Bethel, but it's close by on Route 26. Remember Locke Mills, which you passed on your way to Bethel? This town is home to Ski Mount Abram. The site has thirty-five trails and slopes and sixty condominiums. There is a nursery for young children, a ski shop, rental equipment, and low rates. Since Locke Mills is such a short drive from Bethel, you might find it fun to ski in both places.

When you prefer skating over skiing, you can head to the **Bethel Common.** It is flooded in winter to provide safe skating. People who don't own skates can rent them from the Bethel Inn. There are snowmobiling trails in the Evans Notch/Gilead area, and sleigh rides are offered at Sunday River Ski Resort, the Bethel Inn, and the Telemark Inn and Llama Farm.

You can have pizza at **Rebel Family Restaurant** (207–836–3663) on Route 2. Subs and hot sandwiches are also on the menu. **Mother's** (207–824–2589) is a good spot for families. Open for lunch and dinner on Main Street, this establishment has unique decor and kid-friendly food. Prices are very reasonable. More formal settings include the **Bethel Inn and Country Club** (207–824–2175), the **Sudbury Inn** (207–824–2174), the **Legends at the Summit** (207–824–3500), and **L'Auberge** (207–824–2774).

Finding a place to spend the night in Bethel shouldn't be much of a problem: A lot of facilities are available to you. The **Bethel Spa Motel** (207–824–2989) on Main Street has ten upstairs units over shops. These rooms aren't fancy, but they are clean and comfortable. Priced at around $50 for a double, they are reasonable.

The **River View Motel** (207–824–2808) on Mayville Road is an attractive building that offers thirty-two two-bedroom suites. Each suite has its own kitchen, living room, dining area, and large modern bathroom. One queen-size bed and two twin beds are in each unit. Air conditioning, telephone, maid service, and television are included in the modest room charges. Rates for four guests are about $65 in summer and up to $90 during ski season. As a part of the complex, you can enjoy nature walks along the river, a playground for your children, a whirlpool, a sauna, a tennis court, and a game room. This place gives you a lot of bang for your buck.

Sunday River Ski Area offers a variety of lodging packages. Call (800) 543-2SKI for a complete breakdown. Other accommodations include a variety of inns and bed and breakfast establishments. Rates in the B&Bs range from $45 to $100 a night. Inns typically cost from $70 to more than $100 a night. To get exact rates, call the places listed below:

> **Bethel Inn and Country Club:** (207) 824-2175
> **Telemark Inn:** (207) 836-2703
> **Sunday River Inn:** (207) 824-2410
> **L'Auberge:** (800) 760-2774
> **Sudbury Inn:** (207) 824-2174
> **Chapman Inn:** (207) 824-2657
> **Douglass Place:** (207) 824-2229
> **Ames Place:** (207) 824-3170
> **Holidae House:** (207) 824-3400
> **The Norseman:** (207) 824-2002

Before you leave Bethel, you might enjoy browsing through some shops and stores. A favorite is **Groan and McGurn's Tourist Trap and Craft Outlet** (on Route 2, in West Bethel; 207-836-3645), which has all the stuff you need and a lot of goodies you don't. **Mountainside Country Crafts** (Sunday River Road; 207-824-2518), lives up to its name—you can find crafts galore here. Woodworking fans will enjoy **Meg 'n Gram Shop** (Route 26; 207-824-2948). **Bonnema Potters** (207-824-2821) on Lower Main Street is known for its fabulous stoneware. Many other stores are worth a look. They aren't hard to find, so take your time and explore this mountain town.

RANGELEY

Located north of Bethel, **Rangeley** is the next notable destination for you in western Maine. This is a sportsman's town with a reputation. Fish and animals far outnumber the human residents, and no amusement parks or ocean beaches will attract you here. Good, wholesome fun can be had by nature lovers, but this is not a place for people who only enjoy big-city life. If you want to escape the pressures of urban living, Rangeley is a wonderful place to go.

A trip to Rangeley requires you to meander through a number of smaller towns on your trek to one of Maine's favored wilderness areas. Rangeley is wild, but not as wild as the North Woods. This is a place where you can ski, fish, hike, hunt, or simply relax in nice accommodations. People in Maine are reported to have a special saying that goes like this: "You can't get there from here." You may feel as if this saying is true when you depart Bethel for Rangeley. Fortunately, the route is not as difficult as it may seem. Let me tell you how I would get from the one place to the other.

Going north out of Bethel, take the road marked with three numbers: Route 26, Route 5, and Route 2. This road leads you to the town of Newry and then begins to be marked by only two numbers: Routes 5 and 2. This will take you to Hanover. It's pretty country, so the drive is enjoyable.

When you leave the Hanover (and Rumford Point) area, you take Route 2 through Rumford and then Mexico. In Mexico you will pick up Route 17 for the remainder of your trip up to Rangeley. The region from Mexico to Rangeley has a few interesting activities for you and your kids. One of them is the **Swift River.**

The Swift River is known for its trout and its gold. Yes, I said gold! Real gold that you and your kids can pan for. The gold found along this river is placer–gold, usually in flake form, but some good gold nuggets have also come from the river. Some of the larger ones are displayed in the Maine Museum in Augusta. Rumor has it that one old man lived along the river and supported himself entirely with the gold he panned. Interested? Well, let me tell you how to get started in this fun, and sometimes lucrative, Maine activity.

As you may remember, the friendly people at Perham's Store in West Paris may have sold you some gold panning supplies and books and given you some good free advice. Here's where you're going to use them. Can you really find gold in these parts? I suppose it depends a little on luck and a little on skill, but gold is found regularly in the areas near the towns of Byron and Roxbury. A book called *Bend in the River* was even written on this area and subject. One resource material I checked said that this nation's first gold strike occurred along the Swift River.

Since you will be driving right through gold country on your way to Rangeley, it makes sense to stop and try your luck. Whether you are angling for trout, panning for gold, or just cooling your heels in the pleasant waters of the Swift River, it's a nice diversion from driving. Camping facilities and canoe trips can also be found near Byron. The canoeing can be fast and furious, however, so it may not be wise to arrange a trip with young children. The **Coos Canyon Campground** (207–364–3880) in Byron offers tent sites, swimming, and fishing. The campground is open from mid-April until mid-December. Much of the river is shallow with lots of rocks and ripples. Children enjoy poking around the edges and wading in the shallow water. Good photo opportunities abound here.

When you leave Byron, you should head north on Route 17 toward the Rangeley Lakes. Numerous mountains along the way offer trails that can be hiked. Route 17 brings you into the town of **South Rangeley** near **Rangeley Lake State Park, Rangeley Lake,** and **Mooselookmeguntic Lake,** and **Cupsuptic Lake.** If you and your family enjoy freshwater activities, this is a wonderful place to be.

Rangeley Lake State Park (207–864–3858) contains nearly 700 acres and more than a mile of shoreline along Rangeley Lake. The park opens in mid-May and remains open until early October. Picnic areas are abundant, and swimming is also available. Your kids will enjoy the play area, and there is a boat launch for those who own their own watercraft. Showers and toilets, along with a dumping station for RVs, are also located in the park. Snowmobiling is a favorite winter activity here. A day-use fee of $2 is charged for individuals over the age of twelve.

Moose watching is a very popular activity in Rangeley for both adults and children. You can simply ride around in your car and see a number of the large, brown animals, or you can take a different approach. Rich Gacki is a registered Maine guide who will be happy to show you moose from a canoe. He operates Tuesday, Thursday, and Sunday from memorial Day through mid-October. His trips normally leave from the Rangeley Inn at 51 Main Street at around five in the morning. Trips last about three hours and the cost is $38 for adults (prices vary for children). You are required to make reservations the day before your excursion; call Rich at (207) 864–5136.

Tennis lovers flock to the public courts in downtown Rangeley's Lakeside Park. There are also public courts just outside of Rangeley, in the little village of **Oquossoc** on Route 16 east of Rangeley. Golfers head to

Mingo Springs Golf Course (Proctor Road; 207–864–5021) in Range-ley. Route 4 is the major access road to the links. This eighteen-hole course has club and cart rentals.

Boat tours are a popular attraction in Rangeley. **Expeditions North** (207–864–3622) on Route 17 in Oquossoc has a party boat that tours Rangeley Lake from July through September. The *Queen* (207–247–8053) also cruises the waters of Rangeley Lake. This twenty-passenger boat oper-ates on weekends and leaves the town dock at 1:30 and 3:30 P.M.

Canoeing is always exciting in the Rangeley area. If you want some serious canoe travel, you can take an 8-mile trip from Rangeley to Oquos-soc. Or, you can opt for a longer trip on **Lake Mooselookmeguntic,** where a water trail takes you up to 20 miles around the lake. Canoe rentals are available in the area.

Fish in Rangeley don't just jump in your boat, but they are abundant. Brook trout are the most common catch in the streams, while landlocked salmon are king of the lakes. Numerous camps and lodges in the area offer fishing packages that include lodging, food, and boats. For information call (207) 864–5364. The **Rangeley Region Sport Shop** (Main Street; 207–864–5615) is a good place to load up on tackle, get some free advice, and inspect a list of registered guides who will show you where the fish are. Hours are 9:00 A.M. to 2:00 P.M. every day but Tuesday, when they're closed.

Hiking in this part of Maine can be rugged. There are many good trails for adults and children in good physical condition, but some trails are too challenging for children under six. A 1-mile hike up **Bald Mountain** might be of interest to you if your kids are young. Bald Mountain lies between South Rangeley and Oquossoc on Route 17. Many portions of longer trails can be traversed by young children. It's a good idea to pur-chase a trail guide or talk to a ranger about trail conditions and the advis-ability of hiking with youngsters on specific trails.

If it's snow season when you roll into Rangeley, consider skiing **Saddleback Mountain** (Dallas Hill Road; 207–864–5671). This ski facil-ity can accommodate skiers of all levels of expertise for downhill skiing. The **Nordic Touring Center at Saddleback** (Dallas Hill Road; 207–864–5671) provides plenty of cross-country skiing opportunities.

Where will you eat while in the Rangeley area? Ah, there is much to

No matter what your level of expertise, you'll enjoy exploring the slopes of Saddleback Mountain. (Courtesy Saddleback Ski and Summer Lake Preserve)

consider. The **Rangeley Inn** (51 Main Street; 207–864–3341) in downtown Rangeley will serve you fine food at moderate prices. For a view of the lake, you can dine at the **Country Club Inn** (Country Club Drive; 207–864–3831). The prices are moderate, and the views are spectacular. If you would prefer something a little more casual and less expensive, stop into **Fineally's** (Dallas Hill Road; 207–864–2955). Here you will find a homey atmosphere with a varied menu ranging from Mexican dishes to meatballs. Prices are moderate.

The **White Birch Cafe** (on Main Street at Richardson Avenue; 207–864–5844) is a good place for breakfast or lunch. You can dine on everything from pancakes to seafood, and all the local residents come here, so it must be good. Pizza lovers should eat at the **Red Onion** (Main Street; 207–864–5022), which has great food at good prices. If you are in Oquossoc when your stomach rumbles, try either **The Four Seasons Cafe** (Cary Road; 207–864–5291), or the **Gingerbread House** (Route 4; 207–864–3602). The former offers a full range of dinner specials for two from $29.95; the latter specializes in family-size servings at affordable prices.

Campgrounds are plentiful in the area. One that is both easy to reach and geared for children is **Rangeley Lake State Park** (207–864–3858). Nonresidents of Maine pay $16 a night for a site. In addition to one of the fifty or so campsites in the park, this fee gets you a swimming beach on the lake, boat ramp, picnic sites, and a play area. Other options include the **Cupsuptic Campground** (Route 16; 207–864–5249). Black Brook Cove offers forty-five sites, tenting, electricity and water, a dump station, store, laundry, recreational hall, swimming, boating, fishing, and more.

A variety of rustic camps and lodges are also available in the greater Rangeley area. **Grant's Kennebago Camps** (800–633–4815) in nearby Oquossoc is open from ice-out to late September. When is ice-out? It depends on the temperature, but it is usually sometime in May or sometimes earlier. Situated on **Kennebago Lake,** this camp is 9 miles off Route 16, but you can get there by family car. Cabins are rustic; wood stoves provide heat. Keep the danger of a hot stove in mind with young children. Every cabin has its own dock and boat for your enjoyment. The rates are not

ROGER'S FAVORITE ANNUAL EVENTS IN WESTERN MAINE

Skowhegan State Fair, Skowhegan; 207–474–2947
Western Maine Gem, Mineral, and Jewelry Festival, Bethel;
    207–824–2282
Oosoola Fun Day, Norridgewock; 207–672–4100
Ossipee Valley Fair, South Hiram; 207–793–8434
Mollyockett Day, Bethel; 207–824–2282
Dead River Area Historical Society's Arts and Crafts Festival,
    Stratton; 207–246–2271
Oxford County Agricultural Fair, West Paris; 207–743–2281
Fryeburg Fair, Fryeburg; 207–935–3639
Oxford 250 Nascar Race, Oxford; 207–743–2281
Kingfield Days Celebration, Kingfield; 207–235–2100

inexpensive, but you do get a break on the kids. Adults pay $92 a night, children pay $30. The charge includes three meals, which are hearty. If you can stay for a full week or more, the weekly rate is lower than daily rates.

Bald Mountain Camps (207–864–3671) also in Oquossoc, is open from Memorial Day to Labor Day. Founded in the late 1800s, this camp sports fifteen cabins with fireplaces. The sandy beach is perfect for children, and tennis courts and lawn games are available. The cabins are nestled into the beautiful scenery, right on Mooselookmeguntic Lake. All meals are included. Prices are lower in May and June.

A number of cottages in the area are available for weekly rentals. Rates run from $265 to $750, but a price in the neighborhood of $500 will probably prove to be most typical. Most of the establishments renting cottages offer access to water as well as other amenities. If you want to investigate further, give the following providers a call: **Sundown**

Lodge and Cottages (207) 864–3650; **Hunter Cove** (207) 864–3383; **Mooselookmeguntic House** (207) 864–2962; **Sunset Point Cottages** (207) 864–3712; **Mountain View Cottages** (207) 864–3416; **North Camps** (207) 864–2247; and **Clearwater Sporting Camps** (207) 864–5424.

You might also look into some of the inns in Rangeley. **Rangeley Inn and Motor Lodge** (207–864–3341), where rooms range from $67 to $107, double occupancy, and the **Country Club Inn** (207–864–3831), where rooms range from $144 to $166 double occupancy are both very nice places that offer their own elements of fun and charm. The Rangeley Inn and Motor Lodge is the less expensive of the two.

If I were paying the check, the **Mallory's Bed and Breakfast Inn** (Hyatt Road; 800–722–0397) would be my choice. More in touch with the cost of living for average families (about $72 for a double), Mallory's is open from mid-June to mid-October. This turn-of-the-century estate is on the north shore of Rangeley Lake. Guest rooms are decorated with antiques, and children are welcomed. Lake swimming, canoeing, paddleboats, mountain bikes, and similar activities are available. If you happen to hit the inn during a rainy spell, there is a heated indoor basketball court, two common recreational rooms, books, board games, and television to keep the little warriors occupied. Scenic plane rides are often available, and Mingo Springs, the golf course, is right next door. Pets are considered, so if you have one, ask if it may come with you. To enhance the already attractive lodging package, you can count on family-style rates. Adults pay $55 to $65, double occupancy, daily, with breakfast. Kids twelve and older are $15 extra per child; younger children are charged ten dollars daily; youngsters under the age of two stay for free. From a family point of view, this is a fine choice for a few good nights of lodging.

One other alternative worth considering is the **Northwoods** (207–864–2440). This 1912 house on Main Street in Rangeley offers four guest rooms in the price range of $60 to $75 for a double. Accommodations are plentiful in Rangeley, but they fill up fast, so call ahead for reservations.

Using Rangeley as a base camp or moving out to explore a little more, you can find some interesting activities in the surrounding countryside. The town of **Phillips,** east of Rangeley on Route 4, offers a train ride. Rail fans will be thrilled with the **Sandy River–Rangeley Lakes Railroad** (207–353–8382). Open May through October, the train runs the first and third Sunday of the month. This narrow-gauge railroad was built in 1873 and had an original length of 115 miles. Now you can ride for 1 mile to get a feel for what it was like in the good ole days. The train depot contains an assortment of railroad memorabilia. Fees are $3.00 for adults; $1.50 for children ages six through twelve, and free for younger-than-six would-be conductors.

WELD

The township of **Weld** on Route 142 south of Phillips has a few goodies for the kids. **Mount Blue State Park** (207–585–2347) in the Weld area may be best known for its extensive cross-country skiing trails and 140 miles of snowmobile trails, but its lakeside setting is also perfect for swimming, fishing, hiking, camping, and other summer fun. Campsites, bathhouses, picnic tables, fireplaces, dump stations, boat ramps, and even boat rentals make the park ideal for day or overnight trips. The campsites rent to nonresidents for $12 a night.

Webb Lake, along Route 142 and right along the state park, is a fun place to spend the day. In fact, you may want to spend several days in the Weld area. If you do, give the **Lake Webb House** (207–585–2479) a call. It's also right on Route 142, and the rates are quite reasonable (about $45 to $55 for double occupancy).

CARRABASSET VALLEY

Another area in western Maine worth mentioning is the **Carrabasset Valley** where **Sugarloaf Mountain** is located. If you approach this region from Rangeley, you will take Route 16 to Stratton. There, you will continue on Route 16, which is also Route 27, until you arrive in the valley. If you have wandered down to Phillips from Rangeley, you will leave Phillips on Route 142. This will take you through the town of Salem and into the town of Kingfield. From Kingfield, you will get on the combination route of 16/27 and head into the valley. Maine is a big place with a lot of winding roads, so picking your path is not always easy to do. However, no matter what Mainers say, you can get there from here!

When you arrive in Carrabasset Valley, Sugarloaf will be the center of attention. What is Sugarloaf? Besides being a mountain, it's mostly a ski resort, but there's much more for you and your family to enjoy in this glorious section of western Maine. There are even stops along the way to this haven in the woods that are well worth your time. Let me give you a few examples of roadside goodies along the way.

The **Stanley Museum** (207–265–2729) on School Street in Kingsfield is open all year. Adults are asked to donate $2.00; children donate $1.00. The museum is housed in an old school, circa 1903, that was donated by the Stanley family. The Stanley twins invented the airbrush and found their fortune. In return, they have provided this museum for all to enjoy. When you enter the exhibition, you can study everything from violins to steam cars, which happens to be what the Stanleys are best known for —their Stanley Steamers. The museum is open from 1:00 to 4:00 P.M. Tuesday through Sunday.

The **Western Maine Children's Museum** (207–235–2211) 10 miles from Kingsfield in the Carrabasset Valley is a learning center of sorts for kids. Adults are admitted free; children pay $2.50. Hours of operation are erratic, so call before going. This is a place where children get hands-on activity with computers, science tables, math, a dress-up room, and a real plane. Hours are 1:00 to 5:00 P.M. Saturday, Sunday, and Monday.

The valley is big and includes a lot of fun and entertainment. If you want to rent a mountain bike to explore the area, call **Sugarloaf Mountain Bike Shop** at (207) 237–6998. The shop is open 8:00 A.M. to 4:00 P.M. and also rents snowboards during winter months. For fishing, try **Thayer Pond** at the **Carrabasset Valley Recreation Center** on Route 27. This catch-and-release pond is open to the public. You can get fly-fishing lessons and boat rentals for a nominal fee. This is a good place to introduce your young anglers to the sport of fishing.

Want to play an outstanding eighteen holes of golf? Try the **Sugarloaf Golf Club** (207–237–2000). If golf is not your game, head out for some hiking or swimming. Hiking along **Mount Abraham** and **Bigelow Mountain** is popular for enthusiastic hikers, but the trails can be tough for small youngsters. Call (207) 235–2100 for information. Swimming at **Cathedral Pines** on Route 27 in Stratton is fun for the whole family. This public beach on **Flagstaff Lake** charges you nothing for your enjoyment of the water.

Cross-country skiing is big business in the valley during the snow season. Some folks who can fix you up are the **Carrabasset Valley Ski Touring Center**, with 52 miles of trails (207–237–2000); **Titcomb Mountain Ski Touring Center**, with 12 miles of trails (207–778–9031); and the **Troll Valley Cross-Country Ski and Fitness Center**, with 15 miles of trails (207–778–3656).

If flying down a mountain on two tiny pieces of wood during a snowstorm is your idea of fun, **Sugarloaf/USA** (207–237–2000) is the place to be. Something of an institution in Maine, this outfit was put together in 1955. Today you can find more than 100 trails in the compound. Vertical drops dip from a summit elevation of 2,820 feet. You will probably appreciate the on-site nursery that will take care of your young skiers-to-be while you ski. Instructional programs are available for interested rookies ranging in age from three through adulthood.

If you're in Maine during the snow season and you're looking for something different to do, consider going on a dogsled ride. Yes, you heard me right. **T.A.D. Dog Sled Services,** home of the **White Howling Express** (207–246–4461) will accommodate you. The outfit is in Stratton. You will ride for roughly (and it may be literally a bit of a rough ride) 2 miles. Majestic Samoyeds will pull your sled. A typical run can accommodate two adults and a young child, with ten dogs pulling the toboggan-type sled. Summer fun includes cart rides, so don't write this opportunity off in any season.

If your parental body is feeling the aches and pains of too much childlike activity, you might need to visit a relaxing spa. There's one in Kingfield that is sure to do the trick on the old lumbar muscles. The **Herbert Inn** (Main Street at the corner of Routes 16 and 27; 207–265–2000 or 800–THE–HERB) can fix you right up with a sauna and whirlpool tub. These facilities are rented for $10 an hour.

Sugarloaf Sports and Fitness Center (Main Street; 207–237–2000) is another place you can go to build your body or fix it. This operation is in the **Sugarloaf Inn Resort** in the valley. You can enjoy the following amenities: pool, racquetball courts, hot tubs, steam rooms, whirlpool tubs, saunas, and even a beauty parlor to make you feel better about yourself. Rates range from $72 to $156 per night.

Once you've worked the kinks out and the calories off, you may be hungry. This is not a problem. The only restaurant trouble you will have in the valley area is deciding which establishment to eat in. Eateries are numerous, to say the least. Let me give you a quick rundown of some of your options.

There's a place called **Hugs** (on Route 27 in the valley; 207–237–2392) that is a perfect spot for family eating. Both the food and the service are excellent. **Valley Motel** (on Route 27; 207–235–2730) offers gourmet pizza, terrific seafood, and a children's menu. **D'Ellies** (on Sugarloaf Mountain; 207–237–2490) lets you make your own sandwiches. **The Bag** (also on the mountain; 207–237–2451) offers burgers in a bag. Pizza can also be carried out. If you prefer to eat curly fries and other foods in a booth, you can also eat in the restaurant.

Other places in the vicinity include **The White Wolf** (Main Street; Stratton; 207–246–2922), where breakfast can be purchased for less than a buck, and lunch can cost about $2.00. The dinner menu here starts with a big burger for $3.95 and goes up in price and variety from there. You might try **The Woodsman** (207–265–2561) on Route 27 in Kingfield for breakfast. **Tufulio's** (Valley Crossing Road; 207–235–2010) in the valley, is open after 4:30 P.M. for good Italian food. **The Seasons** (at the Sugarloaf Inn on the mountain; 207–237–2701) serves breakfast and dinner. You certainly have no reason to go hungry with so many fine restaurants nearby.

GENERAL INDEX